Pumping
IVORY

by Robert Dumm

Dedicated to Wolfgang Amadeus Mozart who, in a letter to his father written on January 17, 1778, unwittingly told us all the best way to practice:

"Wherein consists the art of playing prima vista *(sight reading)? To play in the proper tempo, give expression to every note, appoggiatura, etc., tastefully and as they are written, so as to create the impression that the player had composed the piece."*

TABLE OF CONTENTS

MUSICAL PIECES

Cover Illustration: Ricardo Forero. Book Design: Bobbe Stultz. Production Assistance: Barbara Drelles

PREFACE

I hope that this little handbook will help you turn "mind into matter" in practical ways that will make your time at the piano more pleasant and productive. Because practice is a many splendored thing (both doctors and musicians are "in practice" all their lives), each chapter is devoted to just one of its aspects, and is followed by a piece chosen to demonstrate that aspect, edited with a few Practice Pointers to guide you.

You may want to play through all the pieces first, skimming their "pointers" to get the feel of the questions they pose in your mind. Or you may prefer to take each chapter in order, exploring the reasons behind the pointers. Either way, you will find yourself becoming more aware of the music you play, and, thus, will play it more convincingly.

Attitude toward practicing is all important, and just as effective, too. "Wishing will make it so," as the song says, provided you first know how to "divide and conquer." *Wish* the right sounds before each trial. *Wish* yourself to the top of a run. *Wish* your music to be real and from the heart. Those wishes can add up to success if you're patient with yourself, sit down to the piano regularly, and plan, space and score your trials.

Practicing needn't ever be drudgery, nor need it lead to frustration. If you are bored and frustrated, there's something wrong with your procedure or attitude that this book can help you to alter. After all, you're working with music - vibrations that can both stir and soothe your innermost being. This is the art that has been known for ages as the healer of both mental and physical strain; it is the art that furnishes food for the soul.

If you don't like the results you're getting, concentrate on your process: what you intend for that day's practice, and the steps you will take to reach those goals. Frustration arises when a hidden accountant in your brain begins to feel that a fair trial did not net a fair reward. That accountant is budget-wise, and you've got to please him every day. To do this, you must target each repetition so that, however little, it moves ahead to "score."

Section I, "Preparing To Practice," will firm up your attitude, position and critical values, while helping you develop a process that blends both mind and feeling in effective repetitions.

Section II, "A Plan For Practice," moves you right to the piano with a daily plan: what to practice, and how long to spend on each phrase. Proceeding one step at a time, these chapters will lead you through *Warm-ups, Learning a New Piece, Fingering, Continued Work On A Piece, Sight Reading* and *Memorizing.*

Section III delves into your musical impulses, following Mozart's advice to endow every note with the right expression. This is the heart of the book - the part to which I hope you'll want to return after you've read it once, to absorb it as an integral part of your musical thinking. It devotes chapters to *Rhythm, Meter, Accents, Phrasing and Cadencing, Harmonic Rhythm, Key Changes, Dynamics, Tone-Balance, Touch, Tone and Tone Colors, Articulation, Melody Playing* and *Pedaling,* all aimed at awakening the artist in you.

Section IV takes practice onstage to performance, where it has always wanted to go (even if you're shy). It bucks you up as you move through the indispensable tryouts, like stage rehearsals, that make your playing a confident success. Appendixes offer in-depth workshops on several topics.

Bon Voyage! I'll be there if you need me, right by your shoulder, speaking in the same voice and tone I use with my students as we explore together the mountains and valleys of music, day after day, year after glorious year!

Attitude toward practicing is all important.

PREPARING TO PRACTICE

Our opening chapter is dedicated to the young pianist Alan Lee Alder, who recently wrote:

"I am 12 years old, and have played the piano for almost four years. But, for the last year or so, I have found myself sometimes not practicing at all. When I have time to practice, I usually find myself watching T.V. And, when I do play, all I play are songs I know from memory. What should I do?"

Alan Lee Alder, you are not alone. There are thousands of people out there who are fiddling with their bikes (or hair or clothes), or dashing to make just one vital phone call ("after this one call, I'll practice..."). But somehow, that phone call lasts and lasts, or one T.V. show blurs into another, and there's no time left for practice! Even concert pianists sometimes suffer from this condition; in fact, it is a state of mind exemplified in the title which Gary Graffman gave his amusing memoirs, *I Really Should Be Practicing,* a book whose cover photo shows blood on the piano keys.

When the practicing blahs strike, what is called for is an attitude adjustment. You don't have to sweat blood to practice well. You don't even have to think of it as work, or duty, or even something that you ought to do.

Stop a minute and think about it. You *like* music, and you *want* to play some special piece that really means something to you. You want it to sound *through* you - right through your fingertips. Okay? Well, you practice it to *fulfill* that desire, not to frustrate it.

Pause here and ask yourself some questions: What if you could look at a piece of music for the first time, and play it correctly straight off, just as fine as you please? How would you feel about practicing then? Or, what if you were practicing for the Olympic swim meet next year, and felt deep down that you had a chance? How would you feel then about the training? Would you plunge into it each morning? What if you were interrupted at a good point in yesterday's practicing? What if you had just about broken through a tough spot when you had to stop? Would you want to get back to it today as soon as possible?

You answer those questions, honestly, for yourself. There are ways to say "YES!" every day.

But, first, you've got to stop blaming yourself. You don't *have* to be perfect every time. You don't have to be the *best* player, today. And you don't have to listen to what other people say about your playing - people who are only half listening, and don't care the way you do. Put all that out of your mind. What matters is your *desire* to play as well as possible.

Just start with *playing* - one note after another, and keep going. As the Chinese say, "A journey of a thousand miles begins with the first step." And, if the very first step leads to the first slip, be glad for it. You can't, repeat, can*not* learn without mistakes!

Now, start to think more personally about your instrument. The piano, like the guitar, is a "touchy" instrument. Touch it, and you both produce and color its tones, like a potter molding clay. Think of the keys, all gleaming white, as the "skin" of the piano; you can either please them or hurt them. Stroke them, and the sound will come out mellow and purring. Poke them, and the sound will either "bark" sharply or woodenly "thud."

Stop thinking of yourself as playing "on" or "at" the piano. Rather, think of the instrument as an extension of your own body. When an artificial leg is fitted to an amputee, he is then taught to walk *with* it. Gradually, it feels more natural - more like his own leg walking. The French call the keys "les touches," or "touch-points" - as if the keys, not you, were doing the feeling.

Every musician wants to personalize his instrument. Take a look at the vocalist who hugs his guitar, or, without a guitar, woos his mike, or, without a mike, simply woos the audience! Every musician seeks to make his instrument an extension of his own body, the tool he or she needs to put across the strong feelings he has for the music.

Nadia Boulanger, one of this century's greatest teachers, put it best: "Don't speak to me of talent; speak to me of *desire.*" It's what you *want to say* with the music that will create its own technique of expression.

Go to the piano not to reproduce a piece, but to experiment with *your* best way to bring

7

out what is there. There is no one right way to play a piece - no matter how loudly some people protest that there is. Artists, in fact, vary greatly, and audiences return again and again to hear the same piece, as played by pianist X or pianist Y. You simply cannot play a piece twice the same way. Try it! It's like a famous story that gets remade for the movies again and again. There's always a new twist: something you found the last time through that changes things.

Approach your piece like an old-time water dowser. The best of them would travel around, on demand, over drought ridden parts of the country. Using nothing but a stick, they would lightly probe the baked surface of the ground, stopping dead now and then. If a hole was dug at one of those "stop dead" points, a spring of pure water would arise! Go after the "good" parts of a piece: say, the chorus, or a tune that comes later, or a throb of rhythm chords that first caught your attention. "Dowsing" the parts you like best will absorb you in practice. Sometimes, the composer's own idea for the music - what he heard *before* he wrote down the notes - will spring into your head.

Get close to the composer. Help him "come through" to you. Sit quietly, upright and relaxed. Hear the music in your head; hear it ideally, better than life. Sense its movement and pulse rolling through you, turning and adjusting your own pulse. YOU are the prime "instrument" of this music - sitting there alert, tuned by silence, vibrating to its rhythm, lending it your own life entirely. As you feel the music filling you, heart and soul, you will know that it is getting ready to be born.

When it has stirred you, lift your hands to the keyboard. This is the reason you wanted to play in the first place: to bring alive what has already moved you. And, suddenly, by centering your focus, you've turned practicing from a duty into an attraction.

PRACTICE POINTERS

Morning (from Peer Gynt Suite)

1. Roll your hand smoothly, in order to play this figure:

2. The left hand triads throughout are most easily played with fingers 5, 3, 1. This allows the full weight of your hand to sink into the keys, and helps create a full bass sound.
3. In bars 21 to 23 and 30 to 33, hold down the pedal as marked. This is a good example of "sonority pedaling" - pedaling which enriches a harmony, and also allows it to vibrate freely.
4. Follow the dynamic levels carefully. They help the music intensify through the second page, and also project the solo voices above the background.

On the last line of the piece, the *pp* level should show nuances (namely *crescendi* and *decrescendi*), so that the piece does not fade too soon.
5. In bars 48 to 49, notice the *legato* crossover of the left hand to strengthen the final cadence.
6. From bar 49 to bar 50, use an "after touch." That is, catch the second chord (bar 50) halfway up on the rebound of the key action, in order to prevent any break in the sound.

MORNING

Edvard Grieg
(1843-1907)

sonority pedal

sonority pedal

11

2
POSITION AND CONDITION AT THE PIANO

In order to play music, you must first allow it to play you.

Pianists cannot tune their instruments before they play them, though they may wish they could. They can, however, take a moment to mentally and physically tune themselves. To get yourself in tune, sit quietly, close your eyes, and hear the music in your head in the very tempo, mood and manner you think the composer heard in his head. Give yourself entirely to this imagined sound. Let the swing and sway of its rhythm roll around inside you, until you sense yourself moving with it. You see, in order to play the music, you must first allow it to play you.

Such a meditation before you play tunes your mind, harmonizing its activity with bodily action. It also helps you find the right position at the piano. A good position incorporates the repose of the shoulders, the hang of the elbows, the balance of the wrists and the placement of the fingertips upon the keys. A good position also readies the body to respond to the nervous system. Physical tension blocks that freedom. Imbalance anywhere in the body can tighten muscles and interfere with the freedom to play. I think pianists miss the point when they try to control muscles directly. They cannot. It is better to imagine a desired muscular state and telegraph that thought through your nerve network. Trust your muscles; they will respond with a coordination as fine as your vision. Picture, don't will, the movements you want your body to make.

Muscles carry, but do not supply the primary impulse in piano playing, just as phone cables simply carry messages. They carry out commands for the movements of the arms, hands and fingers. Muscles let the arms hang loosely, carry the elbows to a point where they seem to float, flatten or arch the hand, or slightly lift the wrist at the moment that the pianist wants a phrase to breathe. Above all, muscles seat the body in its saddle, holding the torso tall so that the spine aligns its own weight. The weight travels down the thighs and feet into the floor toward the center of the earth's gravity. The trunk muscles, by holding the body in balance, free small muscles for the finer functions of piano playing. These are tiny movements of the elbows and wrists, finger roots and inside the palms. They make the difference between flat and colorful playing. For many years now, ever since you last fell over trying to walk, your large muscles have been accustomed to this balancing act. All you need to do is sit quietly and think balance.

Here are some ways for you to check your position at the piano, and your readiness to move. Refer to them until it becomes a habit, and return to them when you feel yourself tire during practice. If you're very tired, first stand up and stretch your muscles out, slowly twisting your arms.

1. Sit back and sit tall. Don't hug the keyboard. Squeeze in your butt, and suck in your stomach, as if you're a jockey about to urge his horse over a hurdle.
2. Place your feet flat on the floor (the pedal comes later), heels slightly under the edge of your chair or bench. Let your feet feel the floor under you.
3. To free unconscious tension in your shoulders, inhale to fill your lungs. Hold that breath for five seconds, then exhale slowly, and feel your shoulders sinking slowly.
4. Rest your fingers lightly on the keys, and swing your elbows until they hang quietly in an imaginary sling.
5. Still touching the keys lightly, test your wrists with a small vertical motion. Let them settle midway between raised and sunken, either parallel with the key surfaces or up just enough to let the hands hang limply. Don't press the fingertips on the keys.

Once you are settled at the elbows and wrists, your arms will seem weightless; they are in balance. This is the feeling you must preserve as you play, and recover if you lose it. Ludwig Deppe, the great German teacher of the 1870's, described it best when he said "Elbows like lead, wrists like a feather."

The pianist, then, does not practice a fixed position, but, rather, a balanced *readiness to move*. Learn to keep that readiness in the back of your mind, through rests, breaks between movements, and especially at the instant before each new phrase. Retain the notion of imminent flight that is both still and ready, like a bird on his perch. In a sense, we are always perched to play.

And never underestimate the power of a mental picture. Just sitting there reading, registering this parade of images, your inner condition, perhaps even your position, will have changed. A vivid mental picture held clearly in your mind telegraphs immediate muscular changes. Even if your playing is rough and your movements are clumsy, there's nothing necessarily wrong with your wiring. You just need to go back to tuning yourself, thinking the right sound, and finding the motion that creates it. There's no better tuning than "I am ready; here it comes, it sounds like this!" Try it.

Now, confirm this as you play Bürgmüller's *Harmony of the Angels,* a light piece which seems to fly.

PRACTICE POINTERS
Harmony Of The Angels

1. The first two phrases of four bars each unwind to eight bars when the same material repeats at bar 17. Try to play a longer thought there.

2. Practice blocking the chords for a smooth relay between the hands, and an easy dipping of each hand from the wrist.

3. Throughout this piece, hold your wrists a little high - just high enough to let your hands hang like two paws, ready to dip into the keys, or skim sideways on them.

4. In bars 13 - 16, use plenty of left hand tone, as indicated.

5. During the Coda (beginning in bar 25), keep a steady beat, with just a slight *(poco) ritardando* at bar 29.

6. By all means, use the pedal. The markings are to shape each harp-like wave of sound, so lift the foot to breathe.

7. Mark and bring out the left hand thumb in the finger-pedaled chords from bar 25 to bar 28, creating a "slow sundown" line in the tenor voice.

HARMONY OF THE ANGELS
(L'HARMONIE DES ANGES)
OP. 100, NO. 21

J.F.F. Bürgmüller
(1806-1874)

Phrase III

cresc.

p

sf

sf

off

Phrase IV

16

Phrase V

half pedal

half pedal

piů lento (more slowly)

CHAPTER 3

AWAY, DULL DRILL

Good practicing absorbs the player in making and judging sounds. It's not so much a matter of "trial and error" as it is "trial and check." The process is systematic; the attitude patient. The productive inner voice does not say "Darn it, what's wrong?" but rather, "So far, so good. Now what if I play it softer, higher or louder?" The game of practice has infinite variations, and you are free to choose among those your imagination makes available.

I recall rich hours spent observing master teachers at work: Rudolf Serkin with pianists, Pablo Casals with cellists, Pierre Bernac with singers, and Bruno Walter rehearsing the New York Philharmonic. It was always the same: emotions rose, voices were subdued, and the room was electric with expectation. The essential exchanges between teacher and student went on in sounds rather than in words. The trading of sounds was spurred on by small suggestions: "What if we try this?" or "Now. . . much more!" Nothing to interrupt them, this process was repeated until the end of the piece was reached. The practice of music drew the musician and listener both inexorably forward, just as a musical performance does.

But what about repetitions? What about playing a phrase over and over again? In these super-lessons, a simple "take it again" was enough to raise listening to a fever pitch. In fact, not only the student, but everyone present grew donkey ears from listening so hard. Why is it so important to listen? This intense listening advances learning quickly, with a minimum of retakes. Intense listening and honest self-evaluation are the basis of the psychological process behind every successful lesson and every productive practice session. I will diagram it for you, but you must put it into practice.

Here is the process. May it underlie everything you do from here on!

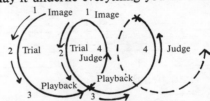

Study what happens with each step of the cycle. Note that you start in the mind, thinking about the sound you want to play. Next, you get ready and play. Then you pause for a mental playback, evaluating the sounds you produced, and, finally, you convert the criticism into a better mental image of the sound. The second time around, you rethink the sound, play it and replay it, and reevaluate it. I call this process the practice spiral, and you're bound to move forward if you use it faithfully. On the other hand, you can dig a deep rut around yourself with unspaced repetitions. Leschetizky, the master teacher, put it this way long ago: "Think twice, and play once."

PRACTICE POINTERS
Waltz from Serenade for Strings - Tchaikovsky

1. This piece was originally written for strings, so this is an "arrangement" for piano. Keep your hand loose to allow for full tones in the right hand, and a sweeping, rhythmic feeling from bar to bar. Create an extra warm tone for the melodic *legato*.

2. Keep the left hand as light as the spring of dancing feet. Each bar should sound like one turn of each bobbing, swaying couple waltzing in a huge ballroom.

3. Bars 21-24 form an extended up-beat. Broaden, but support the tones; the waltz goes on...

4. Pedal for rhythm; press down on the downbeats, lift up for the offbeats.

5. From bar 45 to bar 55, omit the lower octave doubling when you are first learning the notes, and play the upper voice alone. When you add the lower octave doubling, lean into the upper voice.

6. From bar 58 on, practice the right hand in groups with a held pause (for practice only) on the last note of each group.

Why is it so important to listen?

WALTZ FROM THE SERENADE FOR STRINGS

Pyotr Il'yich Tchaikovsky
(1840-1893)

Since self-evaluation during practice is the most important step towards progress, consider what kind of piano critic you are. What do you consider a super performance, a so-so one or a poor one? What do you mean when you say "The technique was fine, but the rest left me cold"? Every year, all over the world, organizations stage major piano competitions to rate and decide the fate of the young pianists who have been "pumping ivory" for the occasion. Artists of international stature huddle in panels of a dozen or more to listen to contestants, compare them and score them. Finally, they pronounce who rates first, second and third, and who does not rate at all. The truth about these competitions is that the judges rarely agree with one another, and the audience often disagrees with all of them.

For each sincere judge, competitions are soul searching ordeals. Judges are artists and they are also human. They know that talent, though not rare, is unique. They can break talent into points of musicianship and technique, but they must leave intact the wholeness of talent - the feeling that somebody is revealing themselves loud and clear in every note they play. Such individuality is mysterious, but its presence is apparent to audiences. Audiences hope to experience that soul baring for an hour or two, and they often make stars of pianists who rated poorly in that competition.

As a judge, I have often faced an official marking sheet which splinters performances. If I give a low mark under "technique," what am I to say under "interpretation"? Is there an impulse to express oneself that somehow emerges through fudgy fingers? There most certainly is! If I rate a contestant's pedaling "unclear," what am I to conclude about his or her phrasing, which seems well conceived, but sounds like a wet noodle? There is a dilemma in judging performances, because wholeness, or the strong impact of personality during performance, can hardly be dissected. Yet, in the struggle of judging technique and musicianship, scores are tallied, averaged, discussed, and prizes are awarded to the "best." Make no mistake, the judges' decisions can make or break careers.

Whether or not your aim is a performance career, you, too, must practice self-criticism to grow at all. It is your tool for advancement. It is the means by which you rate your progress, decide what your strong and weak points are, and fuel yourself for additional tries. During practice, your inner critic must be allowed to comment on each repetition. If you have any sporting blood in your veins, that inner critic will arouse your zeal, and you will probably do better next time.

To call out this critic, play a little game with yourself. Put four small items (buttons, coins, beans, etc.) to one side of the keyboard when you practice a problem section. For every successful trial, move one coin to the other side, until you have "paid your way across." However, for every trial that doesn't succeed, put one coin back where it originally was, and start again with a fresh attitude. You need this honest inner critic.

Be specific about your self-criticism. "Something went wrong" is not specific enough. "Why was my left hand late here" comes closer. You must keep score, even list what went well and what did not. (If you're judging a whole performance, and not just part of a piece, you may want to judge a practice tape-recording. This is a stronger document than your memory is.) Listing problems pins down the details, and helps you decide how to correct them. These decisions, when piled on top of each other, are what make an interpretation yours.

Have courage! After the agony of self-criticism, there's always the ecstasy of success. None of this is dull. The game of self-improvement is the liveliest game of all. The goals are set by your own dreams, and the playing time is determined by your desire to express yourself fully. Below is a checklist that will help you in your self-evaluation. We will consider each of these points in later chapters.

The Piano Critic's Checklist

1. **TONE QUALITY** - The sorts of sounds that reach your ears. Are they full, rich and

The game of self-improvement is the liveliest game of all.

soothing, or are they forced and noisy? Sound is most important since it is the essence of the music, and it conveys the patterns of composition.

2. **RHYTHM** - The movement of the music.

a. Is your tempo right for this piece? (Does the lullaby softly sing and sway; is the march spirited, could I march to it?) When the right tempo has been found, everything, even technique, falls into place.

b. Do you keep a steady beat?

c. Are the intended tempo changes and fluctuations *(accelerando, ritardando,* etc.) clear?

d. Do you return to the original tempo after deviations?

3. **METER** - The measure of rhythm by strong and weak beats.

a. Do you know the time signature (the numbers at the start of the piece)?

b. Do you project a good downbeat for the first few bars? (It helps to conduct your meter - 2/4, 3/4, 6/8 etc. - for at least two bars before you play.)

c. Do you renew the downbeat stresses after accenting other beats, such as offbeats?

d. Are the accents clear, but not so strong that they "rock the boat?"

e. Are the lighter beats of the measure too loud (i.e. beats 2 and 3 in 3/4 time)?

4. **PHRASING** - The thoughts or "sentences" of the music.

a. Do you make each phrase clear, as well as the smaller groupings within them?

b. Is there a clear beginning, middle and end of each phrase? (It helps to place a mark in the center of the phrase).

c. Do you allow each phrase to breathe at its cadence (end), or do you run on?

d. What kind of punctuation is right for this cadence (a light comma, a commanding colon, or a final-sounding period)?

5. **DYNAMICS** - The loud and soft of the music.

a. What extremes of *forte* (loud) and *piano* (soft) are right for this piece? (For instance, *f* and *p* would be the extremes for a minuet, and *ff* and *pp* are the extremes for the entire instrument; remember this is a piano you're playing, not a whole orchestra!)

b. How many degrees can you produce between *piano* and *forte?*

c. Do you animate your smaller groups with dynamic nuances?

6. **TONE BALANCE** - Dynamically balanced upper and lower ranges of the piano.

a. Do your high notes sing out over the bass, or are they drowned out by lower sounds?

b. Can you hear the occasional inner voice when it needs to be heard?

c. Can you notice imitations, that is, the conversation between voices?

d. Are your chords voiced with some tones more prominent than others?

e. Is your overall sound spaced or crowded? Can you sense a dimension between what is out in front and what is background, between the melody and the accompaniment?

7. **TOUCHES** - The tone-colors of the piano.

a. Are your *legato* lines seamless, with tones warm enough to melt into each other?

b. Are your *staccato* notes clearly separated?

c. Do you make a clear separation between touches *(staccato* and *legato)*?

d. Do you have more than one kind of *legato,* such as *legato* and *legatissimo* (the overlap touch)?

e. Do you have more than one kind of *staccato?* Can you play a short and light *staccato,* then a short and biting one?

f. Can you play and notice the differences between a fingers-only touch, a hand touch, a forearm touch and a full arm touch? (This is the way to add more colors in your playing.)

g. Do you try for a varied touch everywhere, especially during sequences and repeated sections (or do all sections sound the same)?

h. Do you wipe out all your touch distinctions with too much pedal?

8. **RESTS** - Those meaningful pauses in the music.

a. Do you cut the sounds exactly where rests are indicated, or do you let them spill over?

b. Do you sense rests as alive, like spoken punctuations, as an indication of more to come?

c. Can you assign different degrees of stoppage to your rests? That is, can you create a gentle cessation of sound as well as an abrupt break in the music?

9. **PEDALING** - The soul of the piano (and its own worst enemy!).

a. Do you crowd pedals, or do you wait until your new sound is clear and fully formed to apply the pedal?

b. Is your pedaling generalized, or is it chosen to enrich special sounds? The latter is more beneficial to your playing.

c. Do you hear noise while you're using the pedals?

d. Why are you using the pedal? For rhythm? To enhance sonority? To connect two sounds or chords? To change the mood? These choices are part of your expression.

e. Do you use the "una corda" pedal (soft pedal) as well as the damper pedal?

f. Do you find yourself unconsciously depending on any one pedal? For instance, do you use the right one for power, and the left one to help "keep it down?" If so, thrust your foot underneath that pedal, so it reminds you of your habit, and proceed to play without it.

10. **ARTICULATION** - Making it clear.

a. In general, does your playing sound vital or tired? Does it seem to be telling us something?

b. Does each phrase have a shape, and does it fit into the whole design of the piece?

c. Do your beats pulse with strong and weak pulses?

d. Does each note, however small, have a definite sound, or are some of them dimmer than the others?

e. Do your notes tend to be clumped together, or are they all separate and unconnected?

f. Is your tone quality muddy or clear?

g. Does a pounding, mechanical sound overwhelm the music?

h. Does a hurrying quality cause your ideas to run together and lose their individual shape?

11. **PRESENCE** - A powerful communicator along with body language and sound.

a. Are you sitting well at the piano, comfortably?

b. Do your movements and gestures grow from the music?

c. Are your movements so extreme that your body loses balance?

d. Put a mirror on the piano and watch your face as you play. What does your face say? Does it communicate strain, or does it change with the music?

e. In a performance, can you lose yourself in the music, or do you catch yourself thinking "What are they thinking?" (Chapter 3, The Practice Process, can help you concentrate on the music.)

f. In a performance, how do you carry yourself to the piano, sit down, position yourself and begin? Afterwards, how do you turn, face your audience, accept their applause and return to your seat? Do you get self-conscious? Don't worry. Presence will come with growing security, and, when it arrives, you'll be too busy thinking "music" to notice!

PRACTICE POINTERS

Sonatina in A Minor

1. The music is dramatic, so play it with fire, but do not play it too forcefully.

2. The dynamic extremes are *forte* (not more) to *piano,* and the contrasts between these levels should be sudden and clear.

3. The composer's slur marks indicate extra warmth to the tone. Otherwise, notes are legato unless marked with dots.

4. Whole phrases are marked with brackets, and given Roman numerals. Try not to interrupt a phrase in your practice, and soon, you'll begin to think as the composer did.

5. Note the different slurring between bars 5 and 30 (note that the second time, the major key is more "singing"). You should usually try to apply this kind of variation to repetitions.

6. Note, too, the different values given the small notes (*appoggiaturas*) at cadences, such as in bars 16, 32, 46 and 64. They point out different degrees of activity at those pauses.

7. At Bar 43, observe the division of the chord between the two hands. This reinforces these climactic chords and causes the rest on the downbeat of bar 44 to seem quite shocking. Support the *forte* through bar 48. This area is the focal point of this musical drama.

SONATINA IN A MINOR

Georg Benda
(1722-1795)

27

CHAPTER 5

RHYTHM: THE DYNAMO OF PRACTICE

You practice to develop the skills to express your musical ideas. In this sense, piano practicing is the same as the training for any sport. Rhythm builds skill and coordinates thought with deed. You need rhythm to coax slow muscles to respond to the quickness of thought. Among all instrumentalists, pianists especially need a keen sense of time to translate their smoothest musical ideas into a series of hammer-like blows.

And it is the timing we are talking about, not the speed! Whether you are practicing or performing, you should dedicate yourself to achieving a clarity which allows ample time for each and every note, down to the smallest note. If you can keep your listeners receiving each and every note (rather than expecting them to understand a flurry of notes), then they will experience the true effect of speed, simply because they are listening so actively. As a performer, you are like a radio transmitter. You must send your "signals" (musical sounds) clearly, with continuous focused energy. This energy is "transmitted" in waves - that is, rhythmic impulses. One of my teachers put it quite simply: "Do nothing in the name of music, nothing in practice, *nothing,* unless you do it *in rhythm.*

The very thoughts of a musician are rhythmic. For example, tap out the opening of Chopin's *Military Polonaise* in A Major, Op. 40.

The very thoughts of a musician are rhythmic.

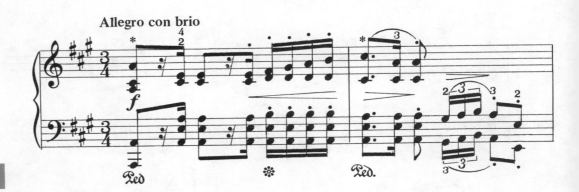

Locate the two main accents of the first phrase (*). Next, tap through the opening again, making the accents very strong. Notice how, when properly accented, the phrase hangs together, and how the notes before and after the second accent seem lighter. You may notice that the sixteenth notes at the end of the first bar seem slightly out of control. If so, you need to inject these notes with more rhythmic energy. Tap a running background of sixteenth notes in your left hand while you sing or just think the rhythm of the theme.

left hand
tapping

Similarly, you can bring any passage under rhythmic control by tapping a running background of its smallest note values. Energizing the small subdivisions of each beat can help you maintain the basic rhythm, even though the note values may be changing. Play through this passage from the second theme of Beethoven's *Für Elise.*

28

You may say "Well, Beethoven has made our job a lot easier by giving us continual 16th notes in the left hand." But, looking ahead, we find 32nd notes in the melody. At the asterisk, the focus of the music is on the 32nd notes. With your left hand, tap out four 32nd notes per beat, and, simultaneously, try to tap out the right hand rhythm. Your patience will pay off in a more settled, less impulsive feeling when you perform these 32nds, and in a graceful, spontaneous feeling at the cross (+).

Get used to tapping out rhythms and subdivisions of the beat so that you can better understand and give life to the rhythms, and feel the subdivisions percolating through you as you play. Pianists often say "You can't play what your ears don't hear." A lightly tapped "percussion practice" is the best way to keep your ears alert to every note. Tap out a problem rhythm with every accent and nuance you intend to play until it's right. Then, while it's still fresh in the ear, try to play it on the piano. If you're not entirely satisfied, stop and try again. Real learning and correction occurs in the ear. What the ear hears and approves, it sends through the fingers.

Make counting a habit, both before and with every move you make on the piano. You could even think "tick-a" for each strong beat, and "tock-a" for each weak beat, thus training your metric sense. For example, a 3/4 bar would be "tick-a, tock-a tock-a." The little "a" (the offbeat) provides a natural spacer for each note. Since one way to think of rhythm is as stress-release, that off-beat is supplying the necessary release. Without a reliable offbeat, you are not sending the listener a complete rhythm. If you do not feel every offbeat, your playing will sound busy and breathless. Since playing offbeats is a problem for many players, try giving them an extra lift by counting "one-then two-then three-then..." It works! It charges each offbeat while you look forward to what comes next. Rhythm is not only the dynamo, it is the powerful spellbinder of music. Once you begin to make a habit of well spaced beats, you will have a good working sense of time. With little effort, you will graduate to having a good phrase sense; that is, the ability to group many measures together in a strong-weak pattern.

Tapping the subdivisions of each beat can also help you figure out and feel any dotted rhythm pattern. For example, here's a dotted eighth-sixteenth melody from Clementi.

Clementi: Allegretto, Sonatina in G major, Op. 36, no. 2

Tapping the rhythm will energize these sixteenths so they sound spirited, not lazy like triplets. You learn what you practice. By tapping out rhythms and thinking a passage through in your head before you play it, you put your brain before your fingers. You train the conductor in you that every pianist must become.

Pianists often ask about using the metronome as an aid to their rhythmic sense. Yes, use it to search for a tempo that works for a piece. Use it occasionally to steady a section you suspect you're rushing or dragging. But if you are not too advanced and use it continuously, you are apt to find yourself fighting it. It's metallic tick interferes with the tones you are trying to hear, which influences the tones you want to hear next. The nagging click of the metronome can lead you to unconsciously force your sound in order to hear better, or to squeeze your tones in between the beats, which defeats the purpose.

Later on, when you've thoroughly learned the notes and skills of a piece, invite the metronome (turned down soft) to play along as the rhythm section of your combo. It should be a fellow player, rather than a drill master.

PRACTICE POINTERS

Arioso

1. The long lines of this piece (only two flowing phrases) make it the ideal choice to use your rhythmic dynamo.
2. As for the upper melody, lean into the first note of each slurred group, in order to both connect the notes and lure the ear onward.
3. The left hand, with its continuous eighth notes, powers the rhythm by placing an almost equal emphasis on the beats and offbeats. Its drive is both subtle and incessant. Keep it very fluid, and dynamically responsive to the right hand's melody. It should shadow the right hand.
4. The dynamic fluctuations are suggestions, but the *crescendo poco a poco* (little by little) will help the long phrase prevail through the slurred group.
5. Between bars 16 and 17, simply transport your right hand over the keys (without a break), but drop your right hand freely onto the third finger at the downbeat of bar 17 (*).

ARIOSO

II
A PLAN FOR PRACTICE — A TIME PLAN CHART

A t the beginning of this book, I quoted Mozart on the subject of sight reading. The first task of the pianist, he wrote, is to "play in the proper tempo"; expression comes next, and then a confident performance. We shall discuss the second two items in future sections, but for now we are practicing to learn the notes, and to learn how to play them in time.

A chart will help you fit the required phases of practice into the time you can spend each day. You may find my time allotments tight, especially if you only have half an hour. You may want to work on the phases tomorrow that you missed today. The important thing is to go through the complete practice cycle, even if it takes several days to do it. There is a certain rhythm to these practice phases. If you alternate intense concentration with more relaxed attention, you will be wide awake and happy. You will be aware of your progress.

The most important thing is that you sit down at the piano every single day, even if it's only for five minutes! Practice is like breathing; it cannot be postponed. It must become a part of your life. By making practice a regular habit, and by setting daily goals and expecting progress, you will find yourself drawn to the piano. Once there, both in mind and body, the music will begin to come alive through you. Here, then, is the chart for daily practice.

Daily Practice Procedure

One Hour	One Half Hour	Phase of Practice
5 minutes	3 minutes	Technical warm-ups
15 min.	7 min.	Learning a new piece
10 min.	5 min.	Continuing work on a piece
10 min.	5 min.	Memorizing a piece
10 min.	5 min.	Sight reading pieces
10 min.	5 min.	Review and repertory
60 minutes	30 minutes	

In this section, I shall devote a chapter to each of these practice phases, plus take time out for two additional chapters - one on fingering and the other on the choreography of your piano playing.

TECHNICAL WARM-UPS: A HALF DOZEN DAILY EXERCISES

Some pianists derive their technical workouts from the pieces that they play, and leave it at that. Others devote too much practice time to technical studies and etudes, long after they have acquired the skills with which the etude is supposed to provide them. I find it best to begin practice with one or two technical warm-ups which work on two balanced skills, working through several keys. As a dancer needs to stretch before dancing, you need to warm up your mind-to-finger coordination, and assure quick muscular response to your brain's commands.

Don't ever think of technique - the special study of motor skills - as divorced from music making. Working on a good trill is an integral part of polishing your Mozart concerto. No exercise in the world is worth anything if it doesn't help you play more fluently and musically. Though all the exercises in this book are original, they are derived from the piano literature. They reduce the movements of playing to individual skills to be learned: octave repetitions, hand rotations, double notes, chords, and five finger action. These are some of the basic skills to be learned. They are accompanied by arpeggios and keyboard shifts, with trills and tremolos as refinements of rotations. These will provide you with a good place to start, and will give your muscles a good, strong warm-up.

I've grouped the essential skills into three pairs, a pair a day. These pairs contrast a large muscle workout with a small muscle workout. All good technical work benefits through the use of opposites, as evidenced by athletics. Stretches are accompanied by releases, contractions are paired with extensions, tension with relaxation. In other words, whatever you do, you should do it in rhythm. And, whenever an exercise permits, work in symmetrical motion; the right hand moving to the right and the left hand moving to the left, both hands going away from (and back to) the center of the keyboard. If you work symmetrically, one brain signal arouses a two-handed response. It's the quickest way to make you into a two-handed pianist.

Whatever you are practicing at a given moment should be cast in a rhythmic framework. I call this "the shape of a skill." Here's a diagram:

Say you want to play a scale without a heavy thumb at the crossover point. You give yourself a mental running start (anticipation) that is several beats long. During this time, you are counting beats and hearing the scale being played fluidly in your head. Then, when you play the scale (action), it will carry itself through the crossover as smoothly as you heard it in your mind. Then, tap out a few beats in tempo as a follow-up, so that you never lose sight of the scale as part of a whole piece of music.

Think about what I just said. You start the beats in your head, not on the keyboard. This is like doing a handspring. You need a running start so you can spring off the ground. The little burst of energy at the takeoff triggers the skill at hand - rolled chord, chord leap, tremolo, whatever - and permits the hand to "fly" lightly to its goal. Don't try to take on too many notes at one time. Divide difficult passages into small groups that make musical sense, then approach each group in the same manner. Don't forget to follow through, so that these individual groups will make sense when you put them all together again.

This is a natural, efficient use of energy which gives your muscles room to breathe. Hands cannot cramp up when you allow them both up beats and follow-throughs for every practice trial. These days, you hear of many professional pianists, in the prime of their careers, who are being forced to stop playing because of muscular strain or, worse, nerve damage. This need not happen. At the root of this problem are bad practice habits - years of unrelieved muscle strain brought about by the thought "There's not enough time!" There *is* enough

Don't ever think of technique as divorced from music making.

time when you work rhythm into your practice sessions, for rhythm truly does much of the work for you.

Stand up tall and do some stretches as a break during practice, whenever you or your muscles feel tired or sore. Stand tall and slowly raise yourself even higher on your tiptoes. Let your arms hang down from your shoulders, and try to make them longer, as if a string were pulling them down to the floor. Then, slowly turn your palms outward. This stretches the muscles opposite to those used in practice. Hold your hands in this position to a count of ten. Then, slowly, return your hands to their normal position. By working your muscles in reverse motion, you have forced tired muscles to let go of stress, and have recharged them with a fresh supply of blood. Work such exercises into your practice routine, and you'll last longer and your concentration will, too.

Here are the three pairs of warm-ups, as promised. They are among those I use with my pupils. They are pairs of large muscle workouts and small muscle workouts, and they relieve tension in every workout. Take each of them through at least six keys, spacing each repetition with some anticipatory upbeats.

PAIR 1 - SMALL MUSCLE ROLLOVERS

Play the same pattern on these pitch-sets:

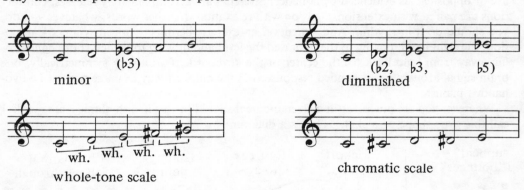

Accent the longer notes.

Reverse: 2x

2x   2x

LARGE MUSCLE OCTAVE EXERCISES

By changing your position for each successive repetition, you get the feel of balancing your weight before playing. After patting the rhythm twice, the third time, it sounds free.

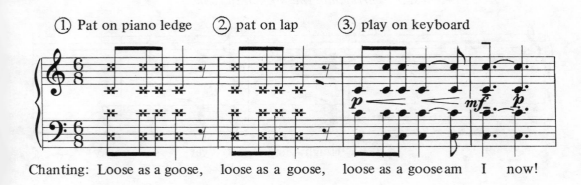

①. Pat on piano ledge   ②. pat on lap   ③. play on keyboard

Chanting: Loose as a goose,   loose as a goose,   loose as a goose am   I   now!

Repeat on each scale step.   and

Both hands: Drip, drop, then one more. Rain on the roof, real-ly com-ing down!

"Gut-ters o - ver - flow, Ev - ry - thing's soak - ing *wet!*

Rub-bers be-long in the hall! Wa - ter is flood - ing the *mall.*"

(Repeat, hands together, up and down *one octave of the scale.)*

PAIR 2 - SMALL MUSCLE FIVE FINGER EXERCISE

"The Lone Ranger"

(Galloping)
(Accent each slur to articulate the broken thirds)

"Heigh - ho Sil - ver, a - way!"

LARGE MUSCLE HAND FLEXORS

Start on step ⑦ *of the scale.*

36

PAIR 3 - SMALL MUSCLE FIVE FINGER EXTENSIONS

1. Lightly "touch" all inversions.

2. "Reach" the second note of each slur.

Apply this pattern to every inversion of the C7 chord.
Then, play it on other 7th chords:

D7   E7   F7   G7   A7   B7

LARGE MUSCLE TRIAD INVERSIONS, DROP AND ROLL HAND ROTATIONS

"Daisy Bell"

diminished   major
triad   triad

Drop freely "melody and accompaniment"

Variation: "Drop and roll" hand-rotations

38

7 MAKE A GOOD IM-PRESS-ION

Consider for a moment how you learn music at the piano. Your brain acts as a computer does, registering sensations from your ears. The ears record every sound they hear, whether you are asleep or awake, and whether the sound they hear is musically right or wrong. The ears and brain will both tend to retain what they hear, especially a first impression, which usually turns out to be an indelible one.

So go easy with a piece you want to learn well. Your ears must work with your fingers (and the ear is quicker than the finger!). You must be aware of the sounds that your fingers are sending to your ears. These same practice sounds are being recorded in your brain. It is what you hear inside your head before you play that guides your hands on the keys. Your ears receive the sounds from your hands, record that sound in your brain, and then your brain tells your hands what to do next. This sound returns to your ear, and the resultant cycle of sound and sensation is extremely important to good practice sessions. Try to always be aware of it.

For good impressions, press each key down firmly, but not so firmly that the key gets jammed into the keybed. Playing like that only dulls the millions of nerve endings in the fingertips. You need these nerve endings to relay information to the brain about the resilience of each key, and the amount of pressure required to get a certain desired sound. Remember the ear-to-hand cycle? You begin by wanting to hear a certain sound, but you must practice creating that sound by using an exact pressure on the keyboard.

Yes, you play the key, but the resilience of the key's action must be allowed to play you *back*. On a good day, the reciprocity between finger and key can become so fine that pianists think of the key as a natural extension of their fingers. It is as though they reached right into the piano to touch its strings, feeling the vibrations of the strings tingling back through their fingertips, and, in reality, they do. The entire piano vibrates when played. You can grow to feel these vibrations, providing you are not pressing your fingertips into numbness.

To further marry your ears to your sense of touch, make some echo tones using after-touches. At each pair of repeated tones, let your finger rest on the first note. Then, replace it with your second finger *without letting the key up all the way.*

> *You begin by wanting to hear a certain sound.*

No break— Not a tie. Repeat the first note with an "after-touch".

Try to find the point on several keys where you can repeat a tone without letting the key up all the way. Notice how rhythmic this process is. You must space the notes evenly, otherwise your music will sound hurried and frantic. This is why you must never work too fast in the early stages of learning a piece, and that is also why you should exaggerate the offbeats between the notes. That off beat provides just enough time to prepare for the next beat and all that it contains.

PRACTICE POINTERS

Rain and Rainbow (from "Children's Pieces" Op. 65, No. 8)

1. In measures 1 and 3, keep the key down for the repeated D's. This should represent a spreading raindrop that "puddles" into the black keys on the third beat.

2. In measure 2, the late pedal after the second beat allows the two tone clusters to merge, then clear with the pedal change.

3. In measure 2 again, the low and high G's of the last two beats of this bar make a "clearing in the rain;" that is, they allow for a relaxation after a certain tension. Other examples of this are at bars 4, 6 and 8.

4. In measure 9, the right hand rainbow theme should be warmly played, but also with a high intensity to balance the deep bass notes. The bass notes, on the weaker beats, should be played with a full sound. This sound should be the product of the weight of your arm, and should then spring up to the middle range, as shown by the slurs.

5. In measure 21, you should lean a little bit on the colorful 9th chord of the third beat. This is representative of the last few drops of rain on the window before the storm clears.

RAIN AND RAINBOW
FROM "CHILDREN'S PIECES"
OP. 65, NO. 8

Sergei Prokofieff
(1891-1953)

The most important thing to remember when learning a new piece is that you should experience it as music, not just a random series of notes. Play through it slowly to understand the layout of the piece, as you would walk through a house and grounds before moving in. Take a slow tempo and keep going. Do not pause for details or mistakes. Leave them and go on. Keep an open mind, and don't make any decisions yet. Simply allow the music to wash over you.

Feel the change as one idea replaces another. Something in the back of your head is registering themes and repetitions, but it is too early to take stock of what is there. Try to register the feelings of things: the character of each theme and the way in which the themes contrast, conflict and resolve. The piece will never seem as fresh and exciting as *now*.

Mozart advised the piano player to work through notes and rhythm to the point where "he must play (the piece) as if he himself had composed it." Keep in mind that your interpretation begins with your first impression.

For your first reading, your dynamics should be neutral, neither too loud nor too soft. Your touch should be *legato*, disregarding any breaks along the way (except for rests). Your brain needs this flow of impressions from your fingertips to create a map of the music. You will probably find that the music will explain itself, given the chance. Even the composer's markings of *Andante* or *Allegro* at the beginning of a piece are no indication of what is completely right for every section of the piece. If the music seems to be more impulsive and joyful at a certain point, register that idea, and go on. Perhaps you encounter a long *crescendo* which seems to warrant an *accelerando* as well. Perhaps there is a conflict between a gentle idea and an aggressive one. The proper tempo will include all these changing characters without letting them overwhelm the music.

So enjoy! Go right on letting the music unfold before you like a movie on a screen. The characters in this movie are musical themes, the events are the interactions between these themes and the scenes are marked by bridge passages, key changes and cadences (closing formulas at the ends of phrases). Music is movement, movement brings on changes, and change sweeps you along. Notice how the long waves (phrases of many bars) will carry you directly to a climactic moment. Keep in mind that the climactic moment of the piece may not be where you think it is. It may very well be a "valley" in the music - that is, a spot where the energy of the piece comes to a dead stop. More often than not, you will be completely aware of the climax of the piece.

After the first run-through, you should map out the music at three levels: phrases, parts of phrases (clauses) and note groups (inside clauses).

Mark each complete phrase in the piece, giving it a number and encircling it with a bracket. Phrases are, more often than not, several bars in length. It is very easy to mistake a half phrase or partial phrase for a complete one. Every phrase has a beginning, a middle and an end. Spoken language can make this clearer. "This morning I went out" is a thought, but not a complete one. You may still wonder why I went out. However, if I say "This morning I went out to buy the paper," I have provided you with a statement which has a beginning, a middle, and an end. Just as the complete sentence is the unit by which all other grammatical ideas are judged, so the musical phrase is the controlling unit in music.

You should also mark the parts of phrases (perhaps two or three per phrase) with a curved dotted line. These parts of phrases express an idea, but not a complete one, much like the clause "This morning I went out."

Finally, you should mark small note groups with small brackets. These groups of notes may be as small as two or three notes. They really don't make sense until they are incorporated into the fabric of the piece. They are the adjectives and prepositional phrases of music.

After you have marked all the phrases and their components, start looking at the cadences at the end of each phrase. Cadences act as punctuation in spoken language, and provide a resting place for the phrase. Try to gauge the importance of each cadence by the

Let the music unfold before you like a movie on a screen.

43

force with which it stops the flow of music. Is it a small cadence, which lets the music run on? Or is it a slightly greater one, which stops the music and announces that a new idea is coming? Or is it the final cadence - one which could be marked with an exclamation point? (Beethoven's music is full of these).

Cadences punctuate music everywhere, not just at the ends of phrases. However slight, they provide a resting place for your ears and your mind. The cadences are where the musical sense sinks in, if, indeed, you want the music to make sense. Decide what sort of break or pause each cadence makes in the musical flow, and mark them accordingly.

If such decisions seem overly fussy, they are the very decisions which will shape the piece as you learn it better. It is important that you figure out these details now, so that your practice time will be productive, and not wasted.

PRACTICE POINTERS

Theme (from Sonata in A Major, K.331)

1. First, you should decide where the whole phrases of the piece are. The song form of the theme leads me to believe that the eight bars of the A strain are one phrase, not two, the B strain (4 bars) is one phrase, and the returning A strain (6 bars worth) is the third phrase. So, the first four bars should be thought of as half a phrase; a clause rather than a sentence, with the active cadence in bar 4 acting as a minor pause in the music. Bars 5 through 8 complete this phrase.

2. Thinking about the sixteenth note subdivisions of each beat before you begin to play will provide the inner pulse for this motive:

You need to be aware of these continuing sixteenths, especially on the second beat of the motive.

3. At the end of bar 7, the *sf* is Mozart's equivalent of an accent mark, telling us to express this chord at about a *mp*, no more. It hints that there is some unrest growing, which flares again at the end of bar 15, and comes to a decisive close at bars 17 and 18. This accounts for the second clause (bars 14 and 15) being compacted from 4 bars to 2.

4. In measures 9 and 10, I've indicated a slight holding of the bass note A's, the sort of "finger pedaling" which was applied by a player in Mozart's time to support the melody.

5. Pedal only as marked (or omit it entirely). In this period of musical history, the pedal was used only to articulate music; that is, to make ideas extra clear, not to add color.

SONATA, A MAJOR
(K. 331)

W. A. Mozart
(1756-1791)

CHAPTER 9

FINGERING

Fingering is best learned by application, but a few basic principles are in order. Chopin anticipated modern pianism and sought to use the fingers according to their individual capabilities. He saw that the fingers act in coordination with the hand, although each has unique characteristics. He did not try to make the fingers equal by isolating them from hand and arm movements.

For example, the middle finger could be relied on to start a phrase or end one. When reaching into the upper register with an outstretched arm, the middle finger could support the weight of the arm. The thumb, since it is opposite to the other fingers, is able to convey movement directly to the keys.

The fourth finger is a problem. It was created weak. Its tendon is connected to that of the third finger, and has to be well trained to play anything more than a passing note. It is not a strong finger, though it can stop a legato run. Chopin's answer to the problem was to avoid the fourth finger, and ask the third and fifth fingers to work overtime, as in the following example.

> *The thumb is the key to a flexible hand.*

Chopin: Nocturne, Eb major, Op. 9, no. 2

You could do worse than to follow Chopin's instincts about each finger's own capability and character. Think of fingers one and three as bone fingers, since they carry direct line action of the arm to the keys. Consider the fifth finger as a frame finger. It cooperates with the thumb. The fifth finger is short, but it need not be weak. It works best in cooperation with the thumb, but it can support the hand and arm weight if used as a vertical pillar. When fingering, use your hand frame - fingers one and five - for the outside notes. Avoid using one and four because their use extends the hand and constricts the wrist. A free wrist can move about, and allow the hand more freedom. Think of a free wrist as your power source for chords.

The thumb is the key to the flexible motion of the hand. It can cramp when held underneath the hand. To unlock this constricting situation, slowly lift your entire arm level with your shoulder. Bobble the arm lightly in this outstretched position. Look at your thumb. It should be hanging freely from your hand. Now, let your arm down slowly and rest it on a table. Let your wrist sink until it lies flat against the table. Notice the relaxed position of your thumb as it lies alongside your hand. Raise your wrist slightly and draw the tips of the fingers along the table top until the thumb touches the index finger. Now all the fingers are ready to play - including the thumb.

Do the following simple actions and observe how your thumb naturally cooperates with your other fingers.

1. Pick up a sheet of paper.
2. Hold a pen and sign your name.
3. Turn a key in a lock.

Note how the thumb works in smooth cooperation with the other fingers.

Watch your thumb work as nature intended by playing this little chromatic scale. (Your left hand should go down from middle C.)

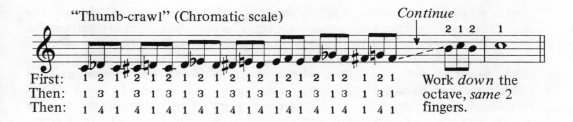

"Thumb-crawl" (Chromatic scale)

Continue

First:	1 2 1 2 1 2 1 2 2 1 2 1 2 1 2 1 2 1 2 1 2 1 2 1
Then:	1 3 1 3 1 3 1 3 1 3 1 3 1 3 1 3 1 3 1 3 1 3 1
Then:	1 4 1 4 1 4 1 4 1 4 1 4 1 4 1 4 1 4 1 4 1 4 1

Work *down* the octave, *same* 2 fingers.

Now that you have worked your thumb with each individual finger, you will be able to play a smoother scale. At first, you should practice playing your scales out from the center of the keyboard in opposite directions. Using the correct fingering for each scale, pause at the end of each finger grouping.

Focus on your thumb and wrist action. You begin each group with a very slight dip of your wrist. Think of it as a "spring-off" such as a runner might feel in his feet. The hand rises slightly to the last note of each group and pauses. It is now ready to dip into the next group of notes. This type of action will loosen your thumb all the way into your wrist. By learning to play scales in this manner, your hand will instinctively begin to dip and rise when faced with small note groups. This action is as vital to musical piano playing as is bowing to a violinist. Watch any great pianist and you will see this circular motion happening in every tempo.

Once you have grouped your scales up and down for two octaves, apply the same principle to arpeggios. I would suggest beginning with seventh chords, because they use four fingers and make your hand turn more smoothly. Practice in this manner:

Next, try triad arpeggios. These will have a gap where the hand slides from your third finger to your thumb. Quite often, this creates a bump or an unwanted accent. Practicing one octave arpeggios before playing the two octave one will give you the running start you need. Remember to aim for the top note.

47

By now, your hands should be getting used to grouping notes by the "handful." The reason for practicing scales and arpeggios is not only because music is full of them, but also because they instill good fingering habits in us. Arpeggios are really only a more open version of a scale; the fingering is the same.

You cannot just clomp through scales by handfuls; you have to refine your touch so that they become smooth and fluid. You may have been taught that accenting the thumb was terribly wrong. It seems that a lot of pianists are unwittingly trained not to play the thumb at all. You were kept busy putting your thumb under, and the rest of your hand over, that your hands became cramped, and your wrists seemed tighter than ever before. It is much better to preserve the looseness of the thumb, always allowing it to hang relaxed beside the rest of the hand. This looseness in your thumb will unlock the rest of your hand as well.

One good way to smooth out your scales is to play them in "wave forms." Try the first example below, and you will see how the oscillation of your wrist keeps your hand loose.

1. "Simple wave"
   Use scale fingerings

2. "Ripples"

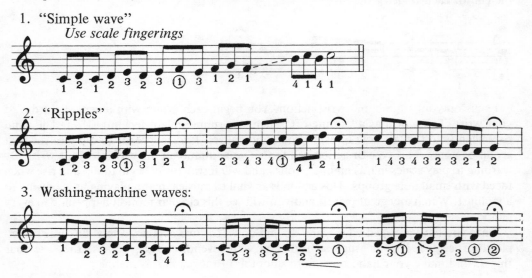

3. Washing-machine waves:

Another important aspect to remember when trying to play smooth scales is that of fitting your fingers to the black and white key arrangement of the piano keyboard. Flatten your hands on a table top. Notice which fingers are longest. These are the ones that will most easily reach the black keys. This is the reason why many pianists keep their third and fourth fingers over the black keys. I train my pupils to always keep their third and fourth fingers over the black keys when playing scales and arpeggios.

Let's look at an F major scale. In light of what we've just said, does the standard fingering for the left hand make sense? No, it doesn't. It forces the third and fourth fingers to cross over the thumb to reach a white key!

It is much better to start with the third finger in the left hand (like all scales with flats), and put the fourth finger where it wants to go: on a black key.

This finger adjustment not only gives the left hand the same fluency as the right, but also allows the fourth fingers of both hands to fall on B flat. The symmetry of this fingering will also help your brain remember and perform the finger patterns much faster.

You will notice that this rule will also apply to the major scales G, D and A. However, it doesn't apply to E Major, because the third and fourth fingers are already positioned over black keys. You will admit that learning this new fingering is a small price to pay for facility in your two-handed scales. I strongly urge you to place the third and fourth fingers over a black key in every scale situation, without exception.

PRACTICE POINTERS

Menuet in C Minor (from the Notebook of Anna Magdelena Bach)

1. The long phrases in this piece (both in the left hand and in the right) should all be played very *legato*.
2. There are three phrases of 8 bars in this piece. The first and last phrases are driven to cadences, while the cadence of the middle phrase is quieter. Try to bring this out in your playing.
3. The fingering has been chosen to further the *legato* lines.
4. In bar 2, both hands change fingers on a repeated note. Use the after-touch we spoke of earlier, keeping the key from rising after the first note. Treat similar instances of repeated notes with the same technique.
5. In measure four, stress the third beat with both hands. This is the beat which links the two clauses of the phrase together.
6. In bars 17 and 18, make sure you use the fingering as written. The 3-1-3-1-3 fingering will help reinforce the climb.
7. From bar 17 to the end, the left hand notes should be separated, but not *staccato*. Think of them as a long staccato.

MENUET, C MINOR
(FROM THE ANNA MAGDALENA BACH BOOK, 1725)

J.S. Bach
(1685-1750)

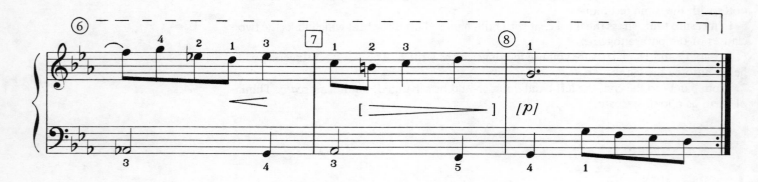

10

MUSIC IN MOTION
(OR 'TWO HANDS DANCING')

After you have chosen a fingering that feels natural, and you can play a piece at a moderate tempo, it is time for the "choreography." Look at your hands as you run through the piece. Your movement should be smooth and connected. Dancers are masters at this, as are actors who, even before they learn their lines, spend time blocking their movements. As they learn their lines, they add gestures to animate their speech. Their goal is the balance of word and motion.

Pianists can learn much from stage people. Think of your hands as dancing on the keys, as two partners embodying the notes in harmonious movement. Watch your hands as you play the left hand of Chopin's Mazurka in B flat (Op. 7, No. 1).

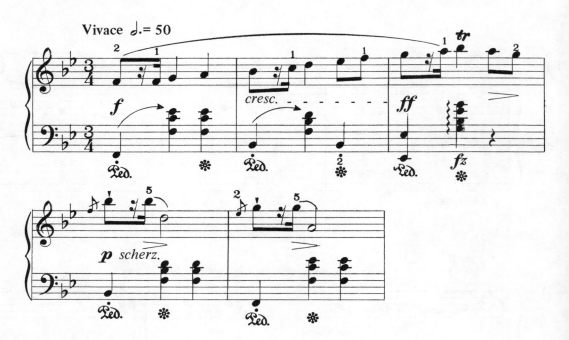

To feel a leap, do we spring off the keys?

You want to give your listener the true spirit of the festive Polish mazurka. The left hand leaps for joy, and this leap should be accompanied by an emphatic dip and rise of your left wrist. Your hand is carried level by a slightly raised wrist, and your arm movements are both up and down and side to side. These are some of the simple, graceful and efficient movements which are part of the art of playing the piano.

The question arises: To feel a leap, do we spring off the keys? NO! You should press your hand into the key action with a quick squeeze. This will release your hand like a spring, giving it the energy necessary to fuel the quick sideways shift.

I would like every pianist to translate their hand gestures into imaginative mental pictures, asking themselves such questions as "What if my hands were actually dancing?" or "What if they were kneeling down to crunch the keys?" Such questioning lies at the edge of technical discovery. Many great pianists have come to think of the actions of their hands as meaningful gestures. Just as a potter's hands mold clay, so a pianist's hands mold music.

The right gesture for the three cadence chords (*) in the example below would be an emphatic down-thump gesture, one for each chord, without leaving the keys.

Schumann: *Knight Rupert,* **from Op. 68**

In our next example, the distant echoes (*) which answer the theme call for a gesture different from that used for the theme. Let your fingers fall fairly lightly from a high wrist.

J. Strauss, Jr.: *The Beautiful Blue Danube*

When you first read through a piece with a broken chord figure, it is best to play them as blocked chords, as seen in Schumann's Little Study Op. 68, No. 14.

Play through it again with the blocked chords, but in the given tempo. This time lean into the keys for the first chord, and lighten up for the second.

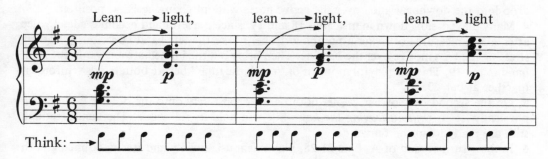

53

Now, play it as it was written, using the broken chord figures, preserving the lean/light gesture as you pass from the left hand to the right hand. The blocking of the chords should have helped the hands cooperate for the smooth transfer of notes from left to right. It always helps to play blocked chords first. Then, when you play the broken chords, the notes will fall evenly into place like the spokes of a turning wheel. If, as you play on, you keep in mind the leaning gesture we discussed, the sound will have an extra added dimension.

You may be asking yourself "Why didn't he just say to play the figure heavy, then light?" That would have been somewhat correct, but very superficial. It wouldn't help you find your way should you encounter similar situations later on. The hands should roll, conveying the motion of the music. The message of the cooperation between hands is richer than the dynamic contraction of finger muscles alone. The difference between these two ideas is similar to the difference between rowing down a stream and drifting.

Run through your newest piece of music from beginning to end, taking note of all the gestures that the music requires you to make. Motion study is not just a matter of labeling; it is the technique which helps you get from one point to another within a certain period of time. If a keyboard shift calls for you to use the first tone or chord as a springboard to the second, you must realize that you may need a little extra time to play the second chord or tone. When practicing, you may allow an extra second for placement of your hands over the second note. When practicing, this second of extra time will be translated into a different stress pattern. You will give the first note a little extra stress, and this will, in turn, allow for slightly more time before you "land" on the upper note.

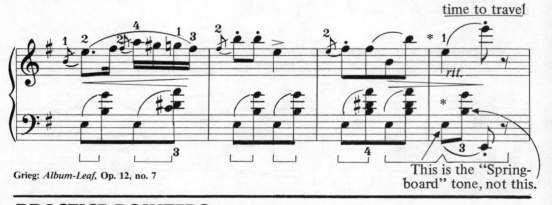

Grieg: *Album-Leaf*, Op. 12, no. 7

This is the "Springboard" tone, not this.

PRACTICE POINTERS

Musette in D Major (from the notebook for Anna Magdalena Bach - 1725)

1. In bar 2, a little conscious stress on both fifth fingers here will help to spring the hands to their next position at bar 3.

2. The same thing occurs on the downbeat of bar 4. A deft little stress of the downbeat will help both hands lighten themselves for their quick outward shift for the downbeat of bar 5. The two beats in each bar renew the up and down dance step. Feel the lift, especially in the last bar of each phrase, which "springs" your hand to the next phrase.

3. Look at the fingering in the right hand of bar 17. Either suggested fingering lets the hand drop into the downbeat and cover the active notes without changing hand position.

4. Many players slow down in measures 18 and 19, since the left hand becomes a lead voice after many measures of being a numbing drone. Make the left hand consciously lead by stressing the bass motive over the bar line. Then bring out the immediate answer in the right hand in bar 19. This is a playful moment of "catch the tune" before both hands reinforce it together at bar 20.

5. On the second beat of bar 20, let both hands drop freely onto the double A, but then physically let go *without leaving the key* while you hold its full value. The hands, though still, are ready to spring outwards.

6. In the return section of A, bars 21-28, play this music openly and freely, bouncing both hands joyfully up and down on the keys. It is, musically, a celebration after the conflict of part B.

MUSETTE

J.S. Bach
(1685-1750)

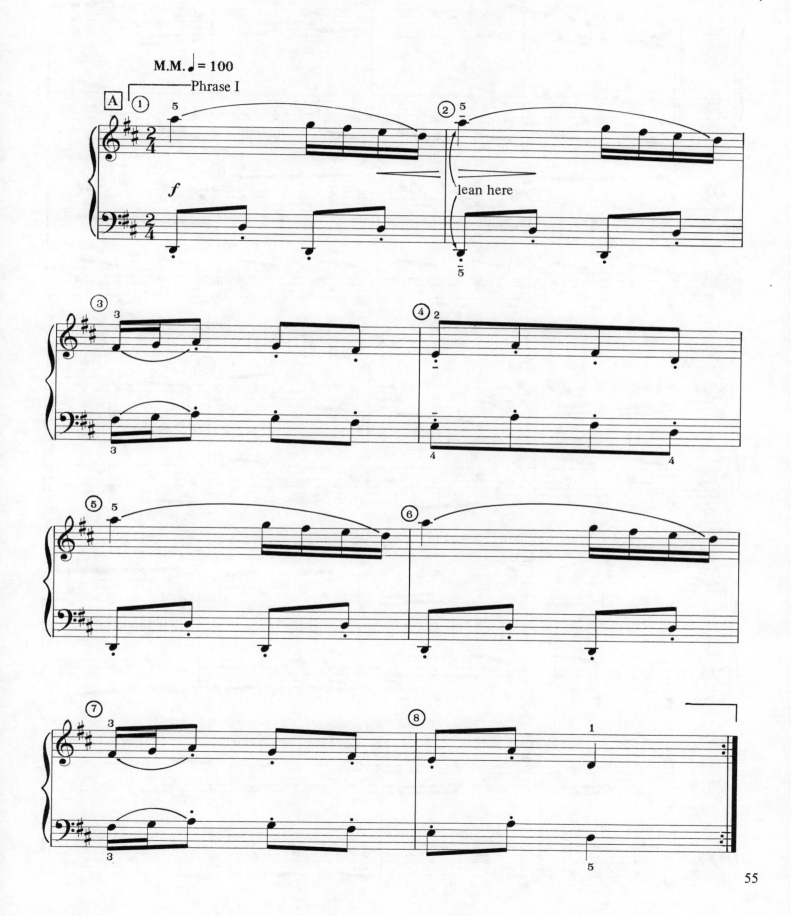

ow long do I work on a piece?'' and ''When is it finished?'' are frequently asked questions. Perhaps the best answer is Mozart's answer. He said a piece is finished ''When you can play it for other people as if you yourself had composed it.'' Since that may take quite some time, we usually settle for playing ''the notes, in time, with some expression.'' When you reach that point, you can let the piece lie idle while you move on to new pieces. New pieces will fuel your burning interest in music, and will also present some of the same challenges you encountered in the ''finished'' piece.

After some time away from the piece, take it out again for review. Whatever problems you had with it may have disappeared because your conception, ability and skill have grown since you last played it. If, however, the problems have not disappeared, then your continued practice will allow you to analyze the problem, divide it up into workable pieces, and, finally, conquer it.

Perhaps you are in the second week of working on a piece. Perhaps there are a few more notes to be learned, but you can play through it on a steady, slow beat. This is good, because now we begin to build on that. Section III of this book will help you do that. It looks more closely at the phrasing, cadences, dynamics, key changes and harmonic rhythm of a piece. We will have to settle for a specific tempo, and suggest how the music will move through its metrics. Pedaling enhances the way music moves, as do touches and tone qualities. We will want to find the breaths and silences which punctuate the music, whether or not it is an official rest. We will also want to be clear about exposed melodies. As we progress, we will get a sense of how individual phrases, if well shaped, can become a part of sections and of the entire piece. Making a clear climax in a piece will deliver a sense of wholeness to your performance. These are all topics which will be discussed in the next part of this book.

Did you get all of it? I can hear some of you asking ''How long does all of this take?'' The artist in me answers (a little too quickly), ''Forever! There's no end to it,'' for this artist in me loves a piece and lives with it, delighting in new perceptions of its beguiling shapes with each fresh listening. If this sounds erotic, that's because it is: you can never get enough of a good thing. However, if we follow our practice chart every day, it is most reasonable to say that three or four weeks is a reasonable period of time in which to prepare an acceptable performance of a piece.

Let's turn now to the Brahms Waltz.

How long does all of this take?

PRACTICE POINTERS

Waltz in A Major, Op. 39, No. 15

First mark the phrases and dynamics of this waltz, taking care to notice the long lines and slow build-up to the cadences. Also note how the harmonies, which change once in every measure, or once every other bar, begin to change more rapidly at the cadence points (measures 7, 14, 21, 28 and 35), resulting in a little "pull" at those spots. Now let's look at a few new facets of this piece.

1. **Touch and Tone Color** - Bring out the top voice of the parallel sixths, especially in the right hand. The dot under the first bass note of each bar does not mean to play *staccato,* as you may think. It means, rather, that you should place emphasis, accompanied by a springing arm and hand gesture, on the note. Until bar 8, it is followed by afterbeats which are very light, and should just drip off your fingertips. This bouncing feeling is characteristic of the waltz.

2. **Metrics** - Since the left hand is "waltzing," that is, generating a heavy-light-light metric pattern, the right hand is free to make the most of the small slurs. In measures 1 and 2, a slight stress can be given to beat three. At cadences, where Brahms makes the right hand heavier (by employing a *portato* touch), you can put weight on both beats two and three.

3. **Tone Balance** is needed throughout the piece, so that the right hand melody balances (matches the sound of) the deep bass notes.

4. From bar 29 on, the **Texture** of the music suddenly widens in the right hand. You can cover this thinning sound by being consistent with the left hand's expression and warmth. This is a magical moment; make the most of it.

5. There are plenty of **silences.** These are not rests, but, rather, they are "breaths" which cannot be ignored. The most effective example of this is the last one at bar 35. Here, you can either pause before the downbeat, or play the downbeat *pp*.

WALTZ, A MAJOR
(COMPOSER'S OWN SIMPLIFICATION)
OP. 39, NO. 15

Johannes Brahms
(1833-1897)

60

I n Italian, *a prima vista* means "at first sight" or "at a glance." Recall that Mozart's first test of a player's capability was the test of his sight-reading ability. What he could not sight-read, he had to practice. This chapter is only a start. You can find more details in Appendix I.

To improve your sight-reading, choose pieces that are at least two levels easier than your repertory pieces. At first, they may appear too easy, but don't be discouraged. Haydn's German Dance which we are going to look at may fool you. To be able to play through the first time, with no breaks or stumbles, requires a certain degree of sight-reading expertise. Why do we need to be good sight-readers? The most obvious answer is that if you are a good sight-reader, you don't need to practice a lot.

Actually, an experienced sight-reader takes in a lot of information at first glance. By the time he does his first play-through, he has already learned many things about the piece. He is already used to spotting the necessary checkpoints.

Let's look at Haydn's German Dance and see what the experienced sight-reader sees.

Don't be discouraged.

German Dance in F Major

1. What is the key of the piece? Look at the key signature just before the time signature at the beginning. You should also look at the very last bass note of the piece, in this case an F, because the same key signature serves for both the major and its relative minor key.
2. Play the F major scale up and down two octaves, playing each tone deliberately. This "tunes" your ear to this key, so you will be more apt to notice a note outside the key of F. This will also remind you of the way the scale lays under your hands, with the fourth fingers of both hands on the B flats.
3. A quick glance over the piece shows that most of the chords are triads (three note chords which are either broken or solid). It is a good idea to play all the triads that this scale can produce. Play a triad for every step of the F major scale.

Scale step: I   Scale step: II

4. Scan the page for the main sections, and notice that they both end in F major (Bars 8 and 20).
5. Scan for accidentals, that is sharps, flats and naturals which do not belong in the key of F major. With experience, you will be able to differentiate between accidentals, (the "promissory notes") and true key changes. For example, the C# in the right hand of bar 6 changes to a C natural on the very next beat, indicating that this is not a bona fide key change.
6. A genuine change of key does happen in bar 11, where the B naturals take the place of the B flat. These B naturals lead the ear to the key of C major. For a beat and a half, we are at home in C major, though the return of the B flat swiftly brings the ear back to F major at the end of bar 12.
7. Even a quick glance at this piece will show you that the melody and harmony of the first two lines repeats itself in the last two lines. Only the middle section, from measure 9 through measure 12, is different. So, the overall design of this piece is ABA.

Keeping these pointers in mind, you should now be able to play this piece, if not at first sight, then at least with valuable second sight. When you play through it, follow these steps:

1. Begin to read slowly and steadily with both hands.

2. If you find it too difficult, play the right hand alone all the way through. The melody in this piece is the guide.

3. Then, play the left hand alone to the double bar in measure 8.

4. Return to the beginning, and play both hands to the same double bar.

5. If the quavering left-hand chords upset your inter-hand coordination, you can block them like this:

Your left hand will then begin to anticipate the next chord.

6. Continue with both hands through the third phrase (bars 9-12). If the action of both hands together confuses you, pat the rhythms out together on the lid of the keyboard.

If you feel that you are hurrying either of the first two quarter notes in the bass, think of, or actually tap out background eighth notes with the other hand. These steady eighths help the coordination of your hands.

7. The three times the right hand starts on the fourth finger in measures 8 through 10 will help establish a muscle memory, while the 1-3-5 fingering in measure 11 lies easily under the hand.

In the left hand of measures 9 through 12, put the fifth finger on the C for all four bars. This helps you find the chord in measure 11 by feel, because it's already under your hand.

8. The trills in measures 4 and 16 need not make you stumble if you a) drop your hand on the first note, b) play the 16ths lightly, and c) give a little "kick" on beat 2, as marked.

These trills were originally written by Haydn like this:

The interpretation of this edition was chosen because the trill fits rhythmically with the left hand.

9. The right hand of bar 2 (and bar 14) is a broken F major chord. You should start this measure with your thumb, so that the other notes fall neatly into place. The best way to get to the thumb without a break is to change fingers on the repeating C of measure 1.

10. From bar 16 to the end, play the melody formed by the thumb notes of the left hand.

This is the melody which you will discover:

Often, by playing the thumb parts alone, you can solve many technical problems. When you add the lower voice, it quite often falls into place.

Now, for a full sight reading workshop, please turn to Appendix I.

GERMAN DANCE, F MAJOR

F. J. Haydn
(1732-1809)

Allegretto M.M. ♩ = 126

verything we have discussed so far in this book relates to memorizing music. There is not one function of the hearing, learning and practice of music that is not memorized as you go. That is why learning must proceed little by little, with purpose, desire and watchful self-criticism. Whatever you do and hear at the piano you *will* remember in the back of your mind, whether it is musically right or not.

I have stressed that first impressions last. This is certainly true, for music at any level. Whatever your ears hear, they record, even if you aren't consciously listening. But if you do intend to recall what you hear, you need to hear *and* listen to the sounds that you are making. You need to consciously listen to the sounds. You can sharpen your listening skills by making many spaced repetitions of the difficult passages before you move on. However, you should not dwell on the difficult passages. You shouldn't upset the rhythm of your practice phases by getting upset about one particular passage. The practice plan introduced at the beginning of this section allows for the ups and downs of our attention span. Don't break your practice rhythm for a small snag. Let it pass by, and start with that problem tomorrow.

Memorizing also helps you move from one frame of mind to the next; from "This is only practicing" to "This is IT - the show must go on." Music always does go on, and thinking ahead often helps you understand the music better. Even when you are doing a practice drill, think ahead to what changes you would like to make in the next repetition. Making necessary repetition creative is the art of practicing.

This is easier said than done, true, but you should begin with short runs. Today, play through a small phrase by heart, and tomorrow play two. Play the same two phrases the day after if you need to. Time is the stuff music is made from, and, usually, time is on your side. Whether you are a professional or an amateur, you should say to yourself, "I have all the time in the world, and this music is beautiful. I will give it the time to grow." Then, give it that time. Observe its growth with pleasure, for the memory recalls best that which it has savored and deeply enjoyed. Anxiety leads to aggressive playing, and this is the downfall of many pianists today, more than you can imagine.

A performer cannot rely on casual repetitions to memorize music. "I play and play, until one day, I have it" is a fool's song. When this fool is faced with an audience, his paradise turns into a nightmare. A performer must be able to start at any place in a piece, and this is why we phrase our new pieces first, to set the framework for the memory. Casual memorizing will not stand the strain of having an audience. The parts you will forget are those which you never knew well in the first place, and the parts you barely get through without forgetting them are the same ones which are erased from your memory with every unexamined repetition.

Before a public performance, everyone should have a few trial runs before friendly people with honest reactions. This will reveal weak spots that never showed up in practice. The Germans have a wonderful word for playing "by heart:" *auswendig-spielen* (to play from the inside out). However, you can't bring out what has never been inside. During practice, your goal should be to shine equal light into every corner of the music, then you can trust it to your ear and your muscle-memory when playing from memory. This spotlighting is best achieved by starting each day with a new phrase, working into a piece, instead of always playing from the beginning.

Most pianists think of memorizing too late in their study of a piece. Memorizing begins with your first careful run-through. It helps to make a small diagram of the piece, a rough copy of the layout and harmonic structure of the piece. Other diagrams that help keep the whole piece in mind are:

1. A numbered list of phrases, each accompanied by a small note, such as "this one plays the same tune, but up an octave."

2. A "fever chart" of the piece, showing the dynamic ups and downs of the phrases on one continuous line.

Memorizing begins with your first run-through.

3. A thick-and-thin chart showing overall changes in texture throughout the piece. It should show the sections which contain close writing with many voices, as well as relatively open writing with fewer voices. This gives you an idea of where the dense textures occur, as well as the more diluted sounds.

4. If you recognize key changes, make a key chart of the piece. Start with a mean line for the tonic key, then show any modulations above or below the tonic by raising or lowering the line.

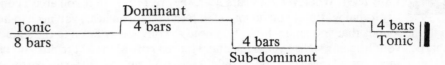

All these ideas are marvelous stimuli for your memory. But you must remember that you play with your body and touch sense. Muscle memories must act out the sounds we hear mentally.

You can help awaken your touch memory by closing your eyes and playing *pp*. Another good way to stimulate your touch memory is to play through the piece on a table top, pressing differently for different dynamic shadings and accents, as you silently play through it in your head. Remember not to squash your fingertips. You should move your hands and arms (the "choreography") along with the music you hear in your head. During this rehearsal, you should try to be very aware of your inner muscular states. If you are poised before a quick shift in register, remember that. If you rest after a powerful accent, remember that. Every day, you should also stand up and conduct the piece (yes, wave your arms around and sing!), to further embody the music. You can even practice just before you go to bed. Play the music over in your head, while you are lying down waiting for sleep. Idealization such as this implants a strong suggestion in your mind for sleep learning.

I have found it helpful to divide a piece into large sections of about a phrase each. Number each section, and begin each day with a new section. Play alternating sections each day. Make sure that when you play a small fragment of a piece, you connect the end of the phrase to the beginning of the next one, but do not go any farther than that. This will keep you from running on.

After you can begin at any starting place in your piece, rehearse playing an entire section without a break. Sing the next section, play the following one, and so on to the end of the piece. The next day, follow the same procedure, but play the sections you previously sang. This is yet another way to learn the music "from inside out."

A few other helpful procedures come to mind. They are:

1. Sing your bass melodies, sometimes playing them an octave higher so you can hear better. If you forget a bass note in performance or practice, it's because you haven't really heard it, or heard how it connects with surrounding notes.

2. Keep changing perspective on a piece. Play the whole piece up an octave, play it faster, play it slower. Play it all staccato and pianissimo, play it in a darkened room for your pet. The last one is important, because you are performing, and someone is listening.

3. Review your tempo plans. Set your opening tempo, plan where you will deviate from that tempo, where you will apply *tempo rubato,* and how long your fermatas will be. Details such as these must not be left to chance.

4. Review the placement of the center of each of the phrases. Mark the center of each phrase, if you haven't already done so.

PRACTICE POINTERS

Minuet in G

The motion of this piece is circular, because a minuet is a graceful circular dance, which is very *legato* and gliding.

1. Notice that the overall design of the piece is ABA. All repeats are taken in the first two sections, but none are taken in the third section.

2. The texture of this piece reinforces the ABA design. The A section is fairly thick and full, and contains many double thirds and sixths in the right hand, and deep bass octaves in the left. The B section employs open spacing, with the space of an octave separating the right and left parts.

3. Through the entire A section, you should bring out the upper voice of each pair of notes.

4. In the bass octaves in bars 13 through 15, play the thumb alone at first, dropping your hand from a very relaxed wrist on every note. Then, let the fifth finger join in.

5. In your music at bar 9, you should mark and be aware of the parallel motion in both hands.

6. Practice the broken chords in the bass (bars 1, 5, 10, 13, 17, 21 and 29-31) as solid blocked chords. This will help you remember the notes.

7. In the right hand broken chords of measures 17 and 18, be sure that you have these chords under your hand before you play them.

8. Be aware of the right hand fingering in measure 23. This will put your hand in position for the A7 chord at the end of the measure.

9. From measures 25 to 29, note how Beethoven uses the highest notes in the left hand to catapult himself back to the tones of the G chord in measure 29.

MINUET IN G

Ludwig van Beethoven
(1770-1827)

① : *All* repeats

② : *Da Capo - no* repeats

Moderato mm ♩ = 96

68

Section **B**

Phrase III

"Heart" of Phrase III

Key of D

Phrase IV

"Heart" of Phrase IV

Da Capo
al Fine

III
EXPRESSION —
"PLAY IT
AGAIN SAM —
WITH FEELING!"

To recall Mozart's words: "Wherein consists the art of playing *prima vista* (at sight)? *To play in the proper tempo, give expression to every note, apoggiatura, tastefully and as they are written,* so as to create the impression that the player had composed the piece." (author's emphasis)

Now that we have learned how to produce a good basic tone quality, let's turn to rhythm, because music begins with rhythm. It is the heartbeat of music. The Russians begin their piano training with good tone production, applying the same somber bell tones to a Bach Minuet as to a Rachmaninoff piece. I have observed seven year olds at the Central Music Schools of Moscow and Leningrad being trained in this manner. Their primary focus of attention was tone and rhythm.

Our examination of musical expression must continue with rhythm - setting the right tempo for a piece, and keeping it steady, so we can feel the manner and mood of the music. Then we shall consider meter, the measuring of the strong and weak beats that bring the time signature to life. Meter is a way to measure rhythm, just as the meter in your house measures the flow of gas or water. We will examine downbeats and after beats, off beats and syncopations. Then we will discuss how to project these factors into our playing, giving it that special vitality.

We will also discuss the projection of meter through the use of accents. Accents which regularly group beats into strong and weak groups are called metric accents. Other types of accents act against the natural pulse of the music, creating the bumps, lurches and surprises that challenge a piece's meter. We will clarify the small temporary distorters of time, such as fermatas and agogic accents.

After the beat patterns (meter) we see in individual measures, phrasing is next in the lengthening series of rhythmic units. Here we truly meet the composer, for composers tend to think of music by phrases. Each phrase must be recognized, and its shape must be mapped and clearly marked. When we understand and play cadences well, we come closer to the definitive performance. In the chapter "More On Phrasing," we will examine and analyze phrases from a variety of different composers.

Much of the movement in a phrase is due to its harmonic rhythm, which is the speed of the chord changes. To understand this action, we will examine the dissonances which spur harmonic progression, often leading a piece into new keys.

Dynamics and tone balance are two things which we will also discuss in this section. Dynamics are one of the things that a pianist can use to arrive at a performance which is solely his own. Tone balance is extremely important; the bass must support the upper voices. Tone balance also includes the ability to make a particular voice, be it inner or outer, stand out from the fabric of the music. Finally, tone balance is needed to differentiate between thick and thin textures; often in a thicker texture we will use less tone and separate the voices.

In Appendix II, we will discuss touches and tone colors, articulation and pedaling. The chapters on melody playing and ornamentation can help your playing be more spontaneous and fluid, while the chapter on rests will show you how to let your music breathe. Being confident in performance, when that performance is not left to chance, is what we will discuss in our final chapter "Practicing for Performance." After all, performance *is* the ultimate goal of practicing.

14 PACE, MANNER AND MOOD

Often, we identify a movement of a sonata by calling it the *Allegro* or the *Adagio*. Those terms tell us that a movement will be played at a certain speed.

Set your metronome for ♩ = 126-138, and pat along with the beats. This is how an *allegro* feels. Now, reset your metronome to ♩ = 69-76, and let your hand wander over the keys, keeping up with the metronome. This tempo is an *Adagio* or an *Adagietto*. While the metronome marking is one of the factors which determine tempo, there are others, which are all rather subtle, but nonetheless important.

The first thing a student will usually ask is "How fast does it go?" This question always makes me pause. Before one can choose a tempo, one has to be able to maintain it. Even if you know the notes, you cannot ride over shaping features like cadences, rallentandos, and fermatas. The right tempo will begin to show itself when you can keep playing the notes steadily, even if they are slow. Take a look at the beginnings of the two Scarlatti Sonatas below. The leaps in the first one would tell me that I need to be able to articulate all the notes, even though the composer has told us that it should be "Not fast, but in dance tempo." For the second example, I would choose a lighter touch and faster tempo to emphasize the running notes.

How fast does it go?

Non presto ma a tempo di ballo

Scarlatti: Sonata, D (K. 430-L.4)

Allegro

Scarlatti: Sonata, Eb (K. 307-L.115)

Tempo is determined by the character of the music. You must try to embody the music, referring to your own movement for the proper tempo. If you want your music to dance, jump, walk or march, your body will tell you the proper tempo. It is true that your first reading of a piece must go slowly, but before you learn it in depth, think about some of these determining factors.

1. Understand the composer's tempo mark. This is usually an Italian word rich in meaning. *Allegro* means fast, true, but it also means happy, high-spirited and upbeat, all of which you can apply to your touch, tone and accent.

2. Watch for the qualifier words such as *cantabile* (singing) or *teneramente*. *Allegro di molto* and *Allegro con brio* are two very different markings. The first means "much quickness," but the second is translated as "fast, with bravura." These markings will affect your gestures, such as the height you raise your hand to just prior to playing an *sfz* or *subito ff*.

3. The metric motives of a piece can determine its tempo. For example, look at this Bach

Three Part Invention.

J.S. Bach: Three-Part Invention (Sinfonia) no. 15, B minor

The sixteenth notes of the right hand are not completely uniform. Bach groups them in groups of three notes each. He changes the first note of each group, while the remaining notes are consistent. The unusual meter of 9/16 tells us two things are going on simultaneously. There are 3 big beats, along with the nine small beats.

As would be expected, you should place more emphasis on the first note of each group of three, and the first group of notes should have a greater emphasis than the other two. Even though this is very structured, you should drop your hand onto each group of notes, letting your fingers do the work, not your arm. This will give your playing an impish quality.

4. The motion of individual voices woven together also affects the tempo. Often, voices are moving at distinct rates of speed, but are woven together, like the small wheels and the large wheels working together inside a clock. You can see this idea illustrated in the *Adagio Cantabile* movement from Beethoven's Sonata Pathétique.

Beethoven: Adagio Cantabile, Sonata ("Pathétique"), C minor, Op. 13

5. Often, two themes with distinctly different characters occupy the same movement or piece. There was a time when a performer could slow down at the appearance of a singing

melody, but that practice is long forgotten. A tempo must be found which is suitable to both themes. In the following example, Beethoven's Sonatina in F major, movement 1, the two themes are distinctly different, yet compatible. The first theme is brash and confident, and the second is pleading and a little hesitant.

6. Phrases, no matter how long they are, must relate to human breathing. If a composer writes a very long "thought," you must move the tempo to hold the phrase together. The example below is a wonderful example of this principle. The music wants to push ahead, yet, at the same time, it wants to hold back. Beethoven has marked it *Adagio sostenuto* (sustained slowness).

Beethoven: Adagio sostenuto, Sonata ("Moonlight"), C# minor, Op. 27, no. 2

More often than not, it is necessary to press the tempo in order to unify a phrase of many small ideas. Here's an example.

Haydn: Allegro Moderato, Sonata, A flat (Hob. XVI/46)

7. Motor patterns are not quite the same as metric motives. Motor patterns suggest a recurrent motion, such as a dance step. The motor pattern in the first two bars of the Schubert Impromptu below suggest a lightness on the first beat. This will lead many pianists to shorten the first beat, whenever this pattern recurs.

Schubert: Impromptu, A flat, Op. 142, no. 2

Later, in the trio section of this movement, we see the "small gear/large gear" movement we discussed a short time ago. This may tempt you to go faster. However, it is a change in mood only. If you hold the quarter notes firmly at an *allegretto* tempo, the lighter texture and longer phrases will make the music seem to fly.

Schubert: Trio from Impromptu, A flat, Op. 142, no. 2

8. As we just saw, a change of the motor pattern in a piece means a change in mood, not tempo. Look at the march below. It moves along in 4/4 time, and smoothly makes the transition into 6/8, where there are three notes per beat.

Howe: "Battle Hymn of the Republic"

There is no change in the pulse, but the unit of pulse switches from a quarter note to a dotted quarter. This is not a tempo change, but, rather, an indication of increasing excitement.

9. When we look at texture and dynamics, we can see that thick writing contains more sound. Since there is more for the ear to take in, you should not play too fast, or use too heavy a touch. A thin texture, however, requires more energy to make the lines come alive. A contrapuntal texture (one with several lines interweaving) needs both extra tone and extra time. In this interesting example, Bach added a trio section to a minuet by Stölzel. While the minuet is spirited, surely an Allegro, the trio cries out for more time with its singing lines. You should settle for an even dialogue between the voices, with an evenly flowing tempo.

MENUET

G.H. Stölzel
(1690-1749)

MENUET TRIO

J.S. Bach
(1685-1750)

10. Tempo and Dynamics are married. Let me give you an example. The larger spaces between notes of an *Adagio* tempo require a louder tone, while a *Gavotte* needs less tone to support it, even though both of these pieces may be marked with a *mf*. In general, a slower tempo requires a warmer tone, while a faster tempo requires a lighter tone. The most challenging tone of all is a warm pianissimo that sings out.

11. Other musicians' perspectives can also lead you to the proper tempo. Mozart cautioned his sister Nannerl "not to play my *Andante* as if it were an *Adagio*." He also advised people to play a fast piece slower, and a slow piece faster. Either way will reveal connecting lines or details you may otherwise miss.

12. Our sense of tempo depends largely upon the sound shapes we hear. For example, I can play this scale very fast, but with no emotion.

Or, I can play it at the same tempo, but with a crescendo to an accent on the last note. The shaped scale, though not actually faster, seems faster because it has more direction.

Now that we have discussed some of the topics which are instrumental (no pun intended) in interpretation, let's look at some of the terms which also influence our interpretation.

Here are some common tempo markings, arranged from the slowest to the fastest: *Lento + Largo* (virtually the same), *Larghetto, Adagio, Adagietto, Andante, Andantino, Moderato, Allegretto, Allegro, Allegro di molto, Vivace, Presto, Prestissimo.*

Next, here are some terms which are used to define the manner or mood of your basic tempo:

Andante teneramente - Tenderly, a little clinging.
Andante con moto - With motion, moving along.
Andante cantabile - Singing.
Allegro non troppo - Not too much.
Allegro assai - Quite, very.
Allegro di molto - Much, very.
Allegro deciso - Marked, with decision.
Allegro molto moderato - Very moderately fast.
Tempo Giusto - In strict time, no deviations.
Tempo Rubato - Literally "robbed time." Expressive stretching of the tempo, without losing sight of the meter. May be applied to a single note, or many notes.

Here are some terms applied to the deviations in tempo. If you slow down or speed up, be sure that you return to the basic tempo where indicated, or in the next phrase. Remember that there may be many slight changes in tempo, but only a few large ones.

The **fermata** (⌒), or hold sign adds time to any note value. Its length is dependent entirely upon the player's wishes (and continuation of the sound).

Accelerando - Getting faster.

Accelerando poco a poco - Getting faster little by little.

Calando - A slight slowing, yielding, giving way.

Piu allegro - More allegro (faster).

Precipitoso - Impetuously; rushed.

Rasch (German) - Lively.

Rallentando - Slowing down.

Ritardando - Slowing down, winding down.

Ritardando molto - Slowing down very much.

Sostenuto - Held back, supported. This term can apply to the tempo by itself, in which case it means "restrained" or held back. Therefore, *Andante sostenuto* means an evenly supported andante. If it is applied to dynamics, it means "continuing or maintaining." An example would be *pianissimo sostenuto*.

Volante - Flying.

CHAPTER 15

METER AND METRIC ACCENTS

The meter will take care of itself.

Most of the music you play is measured by beats, and arranged in bars of strong-to-weak beats. This is the meter of the music, indicated by the numbers at the beginning of the music such as 2/4, 3/4, 4/4 or 6/8. 3/4 meter simply indicates that there are three beats in each measure (indicated by the top number), and the quarter note gets a beat (indicated by the bottom number).

Meter works within rhythm. You will find instances of rhythm without meter, but you will never have meter without rhythm. Meter groups the music into regular patterns of stressed and relaxed beats. It also steadies the forward drive of the music. Tap out a few bars of the 3/4 pattern below. The pattern of accents for each measure is strong-weak-weak. Notice how following the beat pattern steadies the tune (especially in the first measure of this example), even though it naturally wants to favor the second beat.

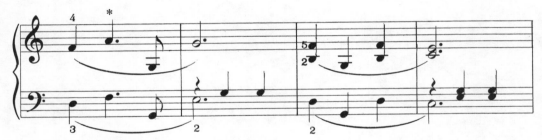

J. Strauss, Jr.: The Emperor Waltz

If you intensify your downbeat stress, the after beats of the bar will accordingly become lighter. Such a stress will add sparkle to the metrical patterns.

Chopin: Polonaise ("Military"), A, Op. 40, no. 1

Waltzes, polonaises, marches and many other movements are written with dance step patterns in mind.

Händel: Sarabande

In the above example, the dancers would step on the first beat of the bar, pause on the second beat, and wait for the downbeat of the following bar. The dance step of the sarabande provides this piece with its metric motive, which, when repeated, quietly provides the musical drive. The sarabande dance pattern underlies many slow movements in triple meter (3/4 or 3/8).

Meters also tend to arrange music by strong and weak measures. This is especially true if the first measure contains repeated notes or chords. For instance, the initial bar of a phrase will seem to be strong, while the following bar tends to sound weaker. This is not to say that you should play it softer, but your ear will hear it as a less emphatic measure.

Beethoven: Allegro, Symphony no. 7, A minor

In this orchestral reduction, the second bar feels slightly weaker. Beethoven, understanding that this would happen, wrote slurs over the "weaker" bars, which was a caution to his string players to play smoothly with no accents. In this dirge-like movement, this strong-weak pattern is repeated countless times, and the effect is spellbinding. Composers often rely on this kind of stress to convey a sense of continuity. The performer must never crowd the beats, or he will destroy the "breathing" effect of this type of music.

Now let's look at some faster music. In this march, see how Sousa uses both stress and line to get you moving to the music.

Marziale (♩ = 120)

Sousa: *Stars & Stripes Forever*

There is nothing static here, even though the meter moves along by half notes, rather than quarter notes. A thumping downbeat stress begins two scales (marked by *'s), which draw you in opposite directions to the doubled G in bar 4. The pull of the scale is strengthened by the syncopation in bar 2. Since dominants lead to the tonic, the G's in bar 4 (with the extra pickup) swing you right into the march tune in bar 5. The tune, which is a repeated "drumming" tone, generates a high degree of forward impulse. Sousa sure knew how to keep us moving!

Open space between voices, speed and negligible metric stress per bar can send music "into space" between strong bars, (*), as in this example.

Pieczonka: Tarantella

The tempo need not be fast in order to span the distance between strong bars. When properly played, the music between the strong bars (*) of this piece should seem suspended, as if in a dream.

Chopin: Valse, A minor, Op. 34, no. 2

In order to establish the meter of a piece, you may find that you need to accent the first few bars. This is perfectly all right, but after a few bars, you should not overaccent the downbeats. The meter will take care of itself. Such is the case in this Gavotte. All you need to do is accent the first two bars. This will define the rhythmic motives, the meter and the tempo. You shouldn't stress them much after that, because that would be as annoying as having a rattle in your air conditioner.

PRACTICE POINTERS

Gavotte II (from English Suite VI in D)

1. Note the time signature that Bach has used. The single "2" means 2/2. This means that there are two beats per measure, and the half note gets a beat.
2. The gavotte step begins with the toe on a weak beat. The dancer steps down onto his or her heel on the downbeat. This explains the presence of the ornament on the downbeat. Bach gives several clues to the importance of this first strong note. The note is a dotted note, which is usually strong. Also, Bach put a slur in the measure. This tells the keyboard player to lean into the first note, and let the others follow. Third, he ornaments the downbeat with a trill, which should be played like this:

3. The eighth notes in the left hand should be played peacefully and fluidly. This is not a jumpy, but, rather, a dignified dance.
4. Notice how the left hand seems to group itself into two bar groups. Add dynamic nuances (as shown) to this part.

GAVOTTE II
(FROM ENGLISH SUITE VI IN D)

84

85

CHAPTER 16

ACCENTS OTHER THAN METRIC ACCENTS

t is against the steady background of metrically patterned beats that other accents express themselves. I call them expressive because they go against the metric pattern; they fight it. They may do this either dynamically or durationally. This means that they may be as loud or louder than the downbeat accent, or they may spread the beats without stopping their sequence. In this chapter, we will speak of *upbeat accents*, which draw attention to a new phrase, and of *displaced accents*, which occur on the weak beats of a measure. We will look at *offbeat accents*, which fall on the weaker part of a beat (the ''and''). These are closely related to *syncopations*, which are strong offbeat accents that cut into a beat and tie it to the next beat. The effect of these accents are varied, as are the names which musicians give them. They account for the ear-catching rhythms you hear. If rhythm is considered the basis of music, the underlying current, then accents are the surface waves which catch the light.

Accents are not neutral. The practicing pianist should locate them, and make sure that they are heard. Here, now, are a few examples.

1. In Kabalevsky's *The Horseman*, the **offbeat accents (*)** are implied by the *forte* dynamic marking. These accents should help the pianist depict the horse's galloping hooves. Throughout the piece, they should maintain their ''kick.''

> *If rhythm is the underlying current, accents are the surface waves.*

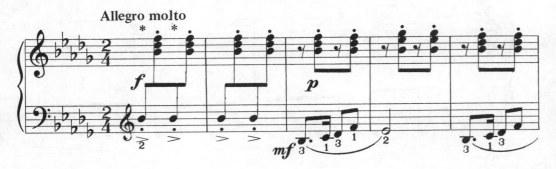

2. **Upbeat accents** often accompany a slight lengthening of those notes which occur on the upbeat. An upbeat, which enters after a rest, is considered to be an accent, because it suddenly catches the listener's ear. If we add a dynamic accent to that normal happening, then we are catapulted into the downbeat of the following bar.

The upbeat can also be prolonged, adding an exaggerated caricature to a downbeat which is already accented.

Et la   tête (et la tête)   A - lou - et - te

"Alouette" (French Canadian Folk-Song)

3. The **fermata**, or hold sign, acts as an accent, as in this trilled fermata from Beethoven's Bagatelle (Opus 126, No.1).

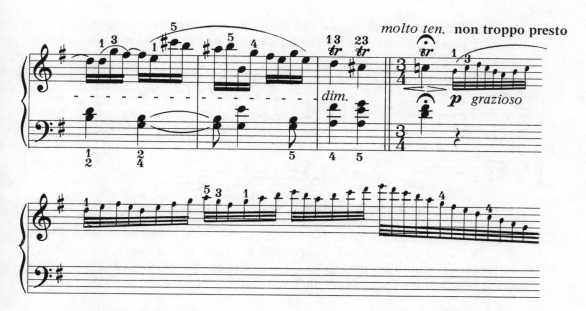

There has to be tonal vitality in the fermata, since it often spills over into a cadenza.

4. **Agogic accents** (I like to call these time-displacement accents) are unique and special, and they should not be overused. Instead of dynamically accenting a note, they accent by displacing or prolonging a note. The result of this type of accent is always increased expression. You stay on the note because you can't bear to leave. It is important to remember that you only stretch - do not break - the rhythm.

Debussy: *La Plus que Lente*

Notice that the note which bears the agogic accent already falls into the section marked by Debussy as *Rubato*.

5. **Displaced** or **weak beat accents** are very lively. You can see what I mean in this example from the Allegretto movement from Bartok's Sonatina.

The displaced accents on the second beats are quite lively here, but throughout the piece prove to be very changeable. The slurs and ties add an even greater weight to the accented notes.

Heller: A Little Song from *The Art of Phrasing* **(1840)**

6. **Syncopations** fall between beats, and urge the music forward with an excited, energetic feeling. They are often tied to the next beat, and also occur in long chains. When this happens, the pianist must mark the regular beats to keep them even. Syncopations are never neutral; composers use them because they want them to be accented.

Beethoven: Allegro, Sonata, F major, Op. 10, no. 2

In the next example, a small boy's ride on a hobby horse is brought to life through Schumann's use of both syncopations (*) and weak beat accents.

Schumann: *Knight of the Hobby-Horse,* Op. 15, no. 9

Even though syncopation occurs in popular as well as classical music, it still sounds best when the syncopated notes are set against a background of regular beats.

B. Bacharach & H. David: "Close to You"

In this next example, the tie after the syncopated note calls for more stress to the normal kick on the third beat of a jazz waltz.

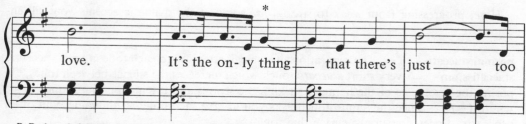

B. Bacharach & H. David: "What the World Needs Now Is Love"

7. The first note of a tied note pair can be considered an accent. This is because that note needs extra tone to carry it through the tied note.

Beethoven: Bagatelle, D major, Op. 119, no. 3

In the above example, there are two things which reinforce the accented tied note: 1) it enters after a rest, and 2) it comes directly after a large leap.

8. **Dynamic accents** can fall anywhere - on the beat, off the beat, or on a weak beat. The effect of these accents is confident, rude, and occasionally shocking, but their tone must never be forced. In the fourth bar of this example, I would play the *fz (sforzando)* loud and sudden. Ordinarily, your accent should be one or two dynamic levels higher (from *p* to *mp* or *mf*). In this case, however, the appearance of outward leaps and added voices justify a more shocking accent.

Schubert: *Moments Musicaux*, F minor, Op. 96, no. 5

Here, progressing from weak to strong, are some of the dynamic accents you will encounter.

normal staccato (·) -   The separations which call attention to each tone are mild accents.
staccatissimo -   A very short *staccato* touch which increases the silence between tones, exposing the resonance of the hammer striking the strings and brightening the sound.
tenuto (–) -   Since the tenuto touch asks you to give each note its full value, you often need extra finger pressure to enrich that tone.
espressivo accent (<) -   This accent is more emphatic than the tenuto. To make the note stand out, you need a definite, conscious pressure of the finger into the key.
marcato and sforzato (sfz) (v) -   These touches are the most sudden and sharp emphases of all; they are a jolt of sound like an electric shock. The key is held by a firm fingertip, while a sudden upthrust of the wrist sends a strong force down into the key (the way you've

seen a piano tuner repeat a note to "get it right").

Sometimes you will find that the *fortes* in the *sforzato* marking have increased to *sfffz* in music at the end of the 19th century. These loud sounds are meant to be an imitation of the orchestral brass. They needn't be savage sounds; remember that it is the piano you are playing.

negative accents - A suddenly soft note or chord where a loud accent is expected. It is often preceded by a hestitation (not a break).

Schumann: *Träumerei,* Op. 15, no. 7

Accents are as varied and expressive as your tone of voice. Using this concept, look at the example below. How many accents would you play, what is their relative strength, and how does the composer clue you in about their placement? (Don't peek at the answers until you've really tried to find them!)

Allegretto quasi Andante
Con una certa espressione parlante

Beethoven: Bagatelle, Op. 33, no. 6

Here's where I think they should be.

1. The upbeat to the first bar has a slight accent. This is the spark to start the music.

2. The downbeat of bar one has a slightly stronger accent. The simultaneous slurs should clue you in to this accent.

3. In bar two, the note marked by a *sf*, plus the ornamental note in the right hand (which falls on the beat, not before it) makes this downbeat twice the size of any of the accents we have seen so far.

4. The trill on the downbeat of the third bar gives it a fairly strong accent, and the slurred group of notes on the second beat gets a very light accent.

5. The downbeat slur in the right hand of bar four makes a medium strong accent. This is the end of the phrase, so the slur should not be too strong.

6. In bars five and six, you must play a stronger right hand to balance the left hand, due to the octave shift. As in the beginning, the separate upbeat should be well articulated, and the slur in bar five asks you to lean into that downbeat.

7. In bar six, the *sf* has more intensity than the *sf* which occurred in measure two. The higher range of the second half of this example exposes the harmonic structure more.

Now you know what I mean when I say "Beethoven is rich in tones of voice."

PRACTICE POINTERS

Scherzo

1. The style of this piece is that of the Italian "tempo di ballo" (compare with Bach's Italian Concerto); beats uncrowded, with springy dance steps. Generally, the dynamics are terraced (play the changes where *marked*), and there should be nuances within those levels of sound.

2. For the best vocal balance, favor the longest note values with the most tone, and give the shorter notes less intensity.

3. Never slip past the syncopations. Let each one prickle your ear and pique your sense of forward movement.

4. Stabilize your time sense by tapping (on a flat surface) the ground beat of the left hand, following that with the offbeat filigrees of the right hand.

5. For every ♩♪ or ♪♩. think: ♫♫

6. Play short trills for neatness and lightness: ♬ or ♬

SCHERZO

With spirit : ♩ = ca. 60-72

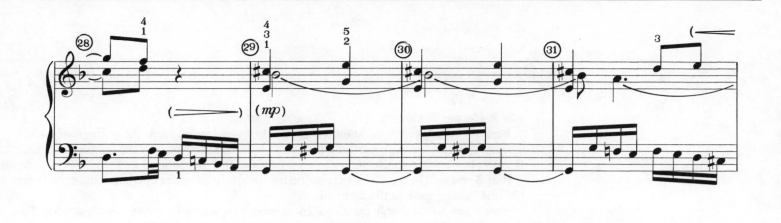

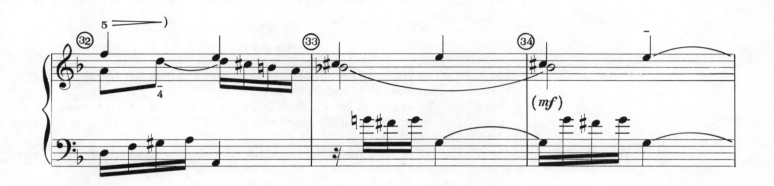

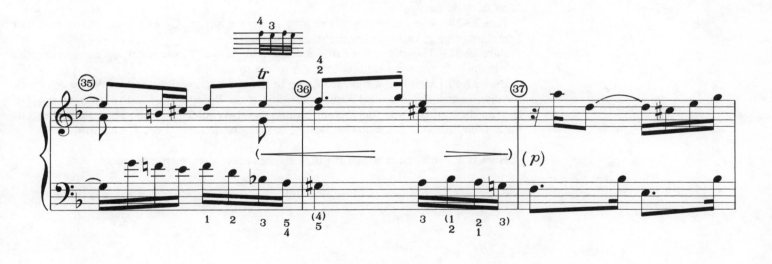

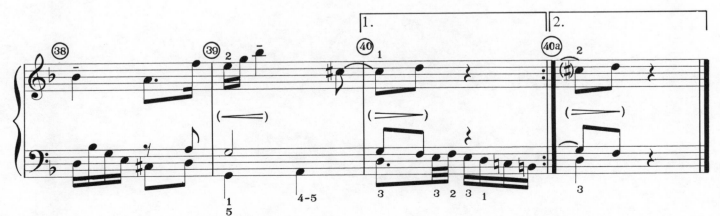

95

The Performer's Analysis

Bars 1-4 - Your left hand should drop on the notes, which form the solid ground-bass. The right hand accents play around the beat. Make sure that you play the tempo as marked. Use a light fingertip touch, making sure to snag each syncopation.

Bars 5 and 6 - The bass 'marks time' on the tonic note *D*, while the right hand repeats the G# (the leading tone to the dominant A).

Bars 7 and 8 - Recharge the alto F by discreetly repeating it on the downbeat of 7. The minor third *(G#-B)* at the end of bar 7 is released by the next third, *A-C.*

Bars 8 and 12 - The key of A minor is implied by these two half cadences on E.

Bar 11 - Slip in the short trill as part of a rising scale melody. Play as shown, or as:

Bar 13-16 - This is a prankish "downturn" of events, and it answers the theme of bars 1-4. Play the upturn at bar 15 with equal zest.

Bars 17-19 - From here to bar 23, Bach insists on his melodic downturn, which is articulated by the sixteenth rest on the second beat of bar 17. Bars 18 and 19 touch lightly on the key of D minor.

Bars 20-22 - The key of D minor rises to G minor, which is the subdominant level. This is a necessary stage of Bach's return to the final tonic level.

Bars 23 and 24 - These bars fan out the dominant seventh chord (containing the leading tone), mark time, and stall the forward movement, damming up the flow of music that will soon burst loose.

Bars 25-28 - The theme brightly returns an octave higher. Give the bass a fat sound and relentless pulse in order to lift the right hand part.

Bars 29-36 - The minor third of *C#-E* stalls the forward movement again, agitating the music until it forces the leading tone *C#* to the tonic *D.*

Bars 37-40 - Maintain a subdued *piano* to the last note, without *ritard.* At bar 39, mark the dissonant *B flat* and the diminished outline of the *B flat* to the *C#* (the leading tone). On the first beat of Bar 40a (the second ending), the two outer parts pile onto the first eighth note, then fade out at the second beat. The sudden silence of beat 2 is a surprise.

Here is an extra piece which features accents other than metric accents.

LE PETIT NÈGRE
(CAKEWALK)

Claude Debussy
(1862-1918)

99

CHAPTER 17

PHRASING AND CADENCES

Recall that, when learning a new piece, we began by bracketing each phrase for the entire piece. We have referred to phrases as sentences. A phrase is as much as you can easily sing on one breath. Let's begin this section by looking at phrase endings, or the *cadence* (from the Latin word *cadens,* meaning "falling"). This falling-off point is where you would drop your voice if you were speaking.

Say the following sentence by Charles Dickens aloud. "It was the best of times, it was the worst of times. . ." Listen to your voice trailing off at the end. This fadeout tells you that the sentence is incomplete, and that there's more to come. It also invites your ear into the silence following the sentence. Read the sentence again with these stresses: "It was the *best* of times, it was the *worst* of times." There is something more settled about your reading when you balance "best" with "worst." It sounds more complete and has a real ending.

Think about your first reading again. Even though its sense of direction is vague, it does convey *some* sense. It contains the voice of a storyteller, mood, emotion, and a perception of something yet to come. You may find yourself listening for and expecting something more. You can see by this sentence that a musical cadence is like a literary cadence; it only partly arrests the flow of the piece. With practice, you will develop a greater perception of just how much or how little each cadence dams the musical flow. Most cadences are very slight, the merest gasp for air while telling a story.

A cadence contains the voice of a storyteller.

Beethoven: *Für Elise*

One can say that every cadence is what the Germans call a *luftpause* (breath pause), or lifting of the hand, whether or not a rest is called for. Cadences punctuate phrases with varying degrees of force, as can be seen in *The Entertainer* by Scott Joplin.

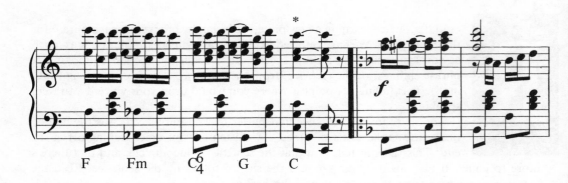

At the first asterisk (*) the music cadences in C major. This is followed by an extended cadence in C. Another extended approach to a cadence can be seen in Edward Elgar's *Pomp and Circumstance*.

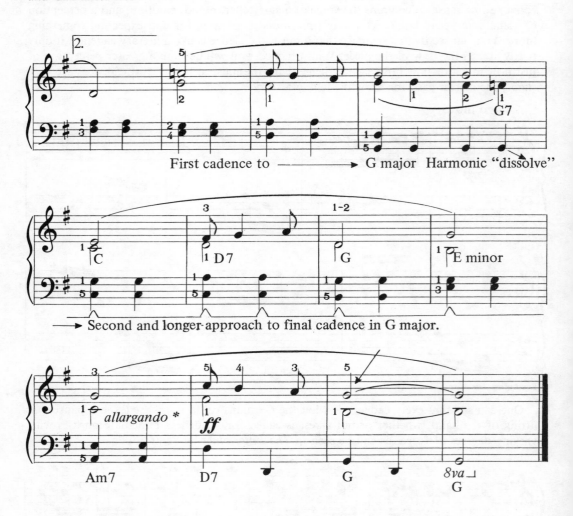

What is often called a "turnaround" is really just a fresh approach to a cadence in the same key. In this piece by Sir Hubert Parry, the turnaround starts in E flat (*) and ends in E flat (**), but look at the expansiveness in between!

Parry: *Jerusalem*

Notice how often a good composer will channel his energy into an important cadence, pulling melodies and harmonies together, creating a denser texture in order to strengthen the stress of the moment.

Schumann: *First Loss,* Op. 68, no. 16

Cadences are spoken of as full and perfect. In contrast, half cadences carry the misnomer "imperfect," due to their non-tonic harmony. For the performer, however, a cadence is a cadence. It should be played strongly, not shied away from, so that it closes a unit of musical sense.

We have been examining cadences which are very strong. Now, let's look at some cadences which are quite the opposite. These are extended cadences which fade away into silence.

103

Rachmaninoff: Prelude, C# minor, ending

In the next two versions of a final cadence, both by Liszt, we catch the composer musing how best to ease his listeners into the silence.

Liszt: *Un Sospiro* **(The Sigh)**

Liszt: *Un Sospiro* (The Sigh)

Notice how the whole tone scale in the bass eases us into the final D-flat chord.

Again and again, you will find that, though a cadence can stop the *sound*, the rhythm which has been built up in the music can go on and on, as we have just seen.

Here are some cadences you will see.

1. **Full cadences** bring a piece to a full stop. This usually occurs at the end of a piece, rarely within, and they usually contain a strong emphasis of a tonic chord. This example has several interior full cadences, giving the piece a dream-like quality.

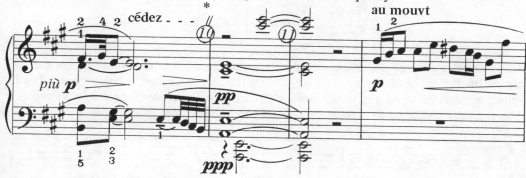

Debussy: *Le Petit Berger* (The Little Shepherd)

2. **Half cadences** are much more common. They are like a semicolon in that they bring harmonic activity to a close, and put you temporarily on hold. They usually end with a dominant chord.

Brahms: Intermezzo, A, Op. 118, no. 2

In the next example, Beethoven's half cadence has a rough sound, reminding us that there's more to come.

Beethoven: Ecossaise (Scottish Dance)

3. The **Plagal Cadence** is a cadence marked by a subdominant to tonic harmony (IV - I). It is recognizable as the cadence which ends hymns. For this reason, it is also called the "Amen" cadence.

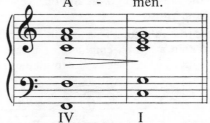

4. A **Deceptive cadence** (sometimes called a "false cadence") is often found near the end of a piece of classical music. It is a musical joke. At the spot in a cadence where a tonic chord should appear, the composer substitutes a chord other than the tonic - usually a VI chord. This is usually followed by a recovery and cadence on the tonic chord.

106

Mozart: Allegro, B flat

With practice, you will learn to tell these cadences apart. Once you have spotted a cadence, play it several times. Try to understand why the composer wanted a stop (and what kind) at this point in the music. This will help your phrases make more sense in relation to each other.

CADENCE POINTERS

Allegro in B flat

It is interesting to note that Mozart wrote this piece at the age of six.

1. In bar 6, the first phrase cadences on a B flat chord. Play this cadence lightly, for there hasn't been any real harmonic action yet, and it's too early for any stopping.

2. In bar 10, there is a deceptive cadence. Notice how the music pretends to be going to the tonic chord, but instead winds up on a VI chord. Two measures later, we are given the cadence we were waiting for.

3. This piece is written in a three part ABA song form. In the returning A section of bar 33, you will notice that the first six bars are identical to those at the beginning of the piece. Notice the bass line in bars 39 and 40. The upward moving bass plus the crescendo make us expect a final cadence, but we are instead given a deceptive cadence. However, in measures 41 and 42, the harmony gets "back on track," and we hear the final cadence we wanted to hear.

ALLEGRO IN B FLAT

W.A. Mozart
(1756-1791)

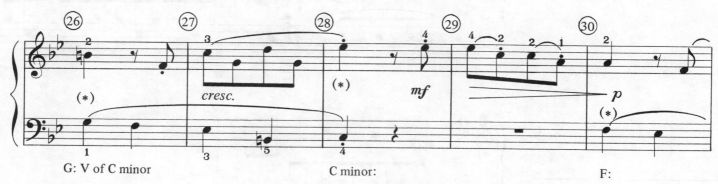

G: V of C minor   C minor: F:

B♭

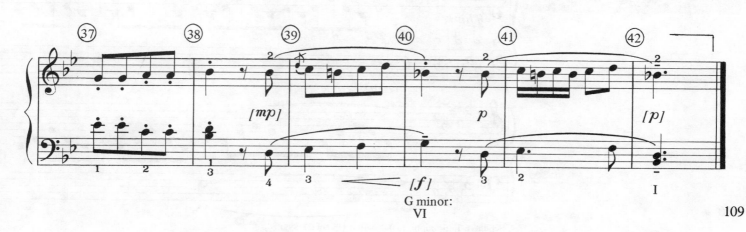

G minor:
VI   I

We began shaping phrases by examining their cadences. Now let's look at two other factors which shape phrases: the start and the heart.

Many phrases begin with an upbeat, which often must be played brightly, to set the mood for the ensuing phrase or piece.

Phrases are shaped in many ways.

Brahms: Rhapsody, G minor, Op. 79, no. 2

If there is no upbeat, you should think through a measure or two in your head. This mental upbeat will give you the proper tempo and mood, especially if the piece is very steady and rhythmic. The time signature of the following example is 4/2, with a feel of two whole notes per measure.

Schubert: Impromptu, G flat major, Op. 90 (D. 899)

Occasionally, a composer will show you the virtues of using a mental upbeat by actually giving you a two measure running start.

Schubert: *Moments Musicaux,* F minor, Op. 94, no. 3 (D. 780)

When there is an upbeat in the midst of a piece, the composer will usually give a moment's pause before the upbeat. This is so that the listener can hear the beginning of the new phrase. You should mark this spot in your music, and be aware of it each time you play.

J.S. Bach: Allemande, Partita No. 1 in B flat

Quite often, this upbeat will have a rhythmic "barb" to alert your ear to the return of the melody (or whatever voice is entering).

Haydn: Allegro con brio, Sonata, C major (Hob. XVI/35)

Sometimes, a mood change within a piece depends on a single upbeat. Make sure that you mark that upbeat clearly.

Beethoven: Rondo, C, Op. 51, no. 1

Many introductions are just long, glorified upbeats. The introduction for Sousa's *Semper Fidelis* march is a perfect example of this. It is nothing more than an extravagant fanfare on *G*. Then, when the "real" upbeat appears in the 8th measure, it, too, is decorated with an *F#* and an *A*.

Every new phrase must present itself as an individual unit, complete from the start. It should seem fresh and spontaneous. Giving it a good beginning, whether it is a substle beginning, as in the Chopin *Ballade* below, or full and vigorous, as in the second example by Beethoven, is one of the mos important aspects of phrasing.

Chopin: First Ballade, G minor, Op. 23

Beethoven: Allegro Vivace, Sonata, G, Op. 31, no. 1

While a clear start and cadence will define the limits of a phrase, you cannot fully bring a phrase to life without projecting its vital area, or "heart." After deciding where this is in my phrases, I mark a heart right into my scores, so neither I nor my listeners will miss it. The heart of a phrase is the most forceful moment, and its most expressive point. It is not always a climax; it may be a sudden silence, or an unexpected change of harmony. There used to be a time when, asked how to find the heart of a phrase, a teacher 1) would tell you their idea, 2) would tell you their teacher's idea, or 3) would throw their hands up and say "You've got to be musical to know where it is!"

The heart of a phrase is not mysterious, but it does vary from phrase to phrase. Every phrase has one. They may be indirect - a whimsical or humorous twist of harmony or melody - these are the subtle ones, difficult to see and hear. You can spend a lifetime looking for them. The point is that you must decide on a heart for each phrase, or you cannot put that phrase across musically. Not having a heart in your phrase is like having to explain a joke - it loses something in the translation.

Let's look at some phrases and point out the hearts. Sometimes the heart is easy to spot.

Mozart: Allegro (theme), Sonata, C (K. 545)

The slur mark that Mozart placed on the dotted note downbeat makes the B in bar 2 very strong. You might be tempted to place your heart at (*), but you shouldn't. Doing so would make two phrases out of what is really only one, and would give your performance a sing-song effect very unbecoming to this work.

Sometimes you must conduct the music silently, and look to the end of a phrase to find its heart, or, as before, you will end up giving more than one heart to the phrase, which is an unnatural situation.

Haydn: Scherzo, F major (opening)

As I mentioned before, the heart of the phrase need not be a loud place, or even a sound. It can be the opposite, where the sound, for a suspended second, nearly dies.

114

Chopin: Prelude, E minor, Op. 28, no. 4

In the above example, the "stop" is the single rest of the piece, making it not only the heart of this phrase, but the heart of the entire piece.

The heart is not always concentrated in one or two beats. Sometimes it appears as a "bleeding heart," spread out over a fairly large area.

Chopin: Valse, C# minor, Op. 64, no. 2

In the following case, the eight bar phrase has one heart, but it is spread out over the last two bars. You will want to give a little extra life to the "artery" in bar 4 (*), which animates the first four bars.

115

Schubert: Impromptu, B flat major, Op. 142, no. 3 (D. 935)

Once you have found the heart of the phrase, then be sure to reserve your energy to better project that area. Underplay low-energy areas, and your phrases will have better shape and propulsion.

Schubert: Fantasy Sonata, G, Op. 78 (D. 894)

There you have it. You now know the three points for shaping a phrase: the start, the heart and the cadence. By making each phrase clear at all three points, you will bring it to life in a way you never dreamed possible. Here, then, are two points to remember.
1) Phrase repetitions should be varied. This is excellent advice. You cannot change the start or ending of a phrase, but you can change the placement of the heart. It is a good idea to move the heart a little closer to the end of the phrase when you repeat, to push the music into the next phrase.

First time: ♡ "Heart" of phrase

Second time: ♡ Heart goes here

J.S. Bach: Musette

2) Sequences are close repetitions of melodic or harmonic fragments. The danger of boring sameness is increased in a sequence, since all the fragments have the same pitch shape, and the only difference is that they are up or down a step or two. Dynamic variation is your only freedom of expression, so you should not only mark the heart of each short "phraselet" in the sequence, but change its position for each one.

Sequence ①

Mozart: Fantasy, C minor (K. 475)

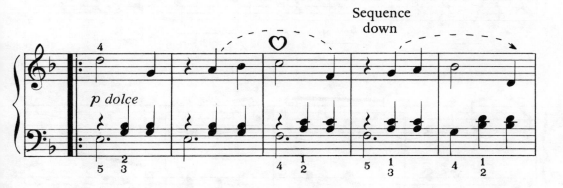

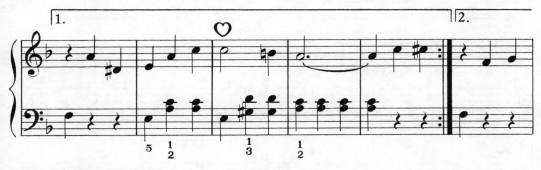

Tchaikovsky: Waltz of the Flowers

In addition to the aforementioned change in location of the heart, you can also spread out the heart during the repetition.

Puccini: Musetta's Waltz Song (from "La Bohème")

PRACTICE POINTERS

Of Foreign Lands and People ("from Scenes from Childhood")
Op. 15.

1. It is interesting to note that this is the original version, taken from the first edition. All the markings are Schumann's.

2. Make sure you take all the repeats in this piece. The second time through a section, try to vary it in some way. You can use a different dynamic level, you can move the heart of the phrase a little, or you can linger on a tone (see 'Agogic accents' in Chapter 16).

3. In bars 1 through 8, Schumann uses the "law of three." Notice how he groups the musical clauses in this 8 measure phrase. The grouping is:

```
┌Phrase I  - - - - - →                    ┐
  ⌒⌒⌒⌒⌒       ⌒⌒⌒⌒⌒        ⌒⌒⌒⌒⌒
  2 bars   +   2 bars   +   4 bars
  short - - - - - short - - - - - lo-o-ong
```

Since this is the phrase structure for the entire piece, try to incorporate it into your interpretation.

4. The heart of each of these phrases lies in the long, 4-bar clause of each phrase. I have marked the location of each.

5. Relocate the heart of each phrase slightly for each repeat. When you've decided where it will be, mark it in the music.

OF FOREIGN LANDS AND PEOPLE
(FROM "SCENES FROM CHILDHOOD," OP. 15)

Robert Schumann
(1810-1856)

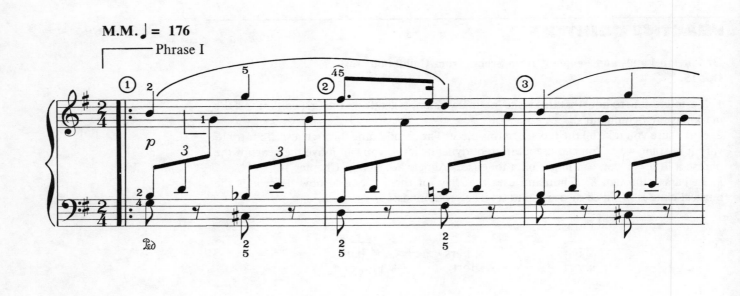

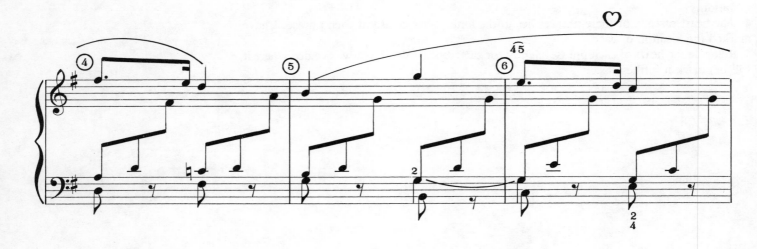

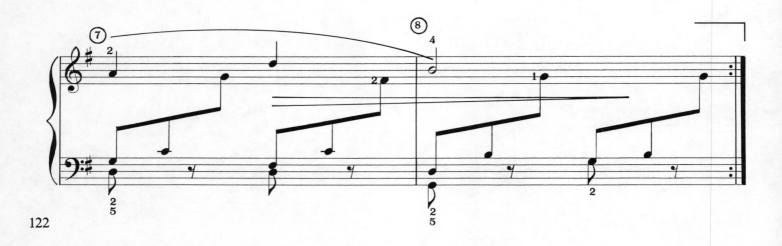

CHAPTER 19

HARMONIC RHYTHM

nderstanding the harmonic rhythm of music can help you shape your phrases. The tension in most phrases is built slowly, and this is usually due to the harmonic rhythm, and is emphasized by the dynamics in the phrase. Harmonic rhythm is the speed with which chords change from one to another. Usually, the rhythm at the start of a phrase is slow, changing every other beat, or, as in the example below, every beat. Then, as we get closer to the cadence, the chords change faster, usually doubling their rate of speed. (Don't worry if you don't know what the chords are, just try to sense where they change.) In this example, the harmonic rhythm has been marked under the score.

Händel: Theme from Harmonious Blacksmith Variations

Until the cadence, the chord changes are synchronized with the metric rhythm. Then they get faster two beats before the final chord, signaling that a cadence is coming. At the cadence, the growing tension is relieved, and we are free to start a new phrase.

A good composer builds tension in phrases in many ways; by increasing dynamic levels, by thickening the voices, or spreading them farther apart, by adding more dissonant harmony, or by promising a key change. The player must help energize the building tension, never allowing it to "deflate" before the cadence. Practice the art of tension building by directing your intensity toward the peak area, often the next to last chord of a cadence, that is, the chord just prior to the release of the tension. By adding fine dynamic changes and little tempo fluctuations, you can hint at what is yet to come. What comes is the cadence, and even that cadence can be part of a larger series of cadences which grows in intensity until we reach the final one.

Now, let's look at harmonic progressions and their influence on harmonic rhythm. Play these two chords.

When you stopped on the second chord, you probably felt a certain tension, a feeling that the musical statement wasn't finished. Now play this series of chords.

> *A player must help energize the building musical tension.*

Compare these two sets of chords. You will notice that the second set seems to be more finished; it has rid itself of the tension. The *dissonance* in the first example has been resolved to a *consonance* in the second.

Here is a series of chords. Play them softly and slowly, listening carefully. Try to hear which chords have the greatest "pull," that is, those which seem unresolved.

1. Scale-step of chord root: I   vi   IV   ii   V7   I
2. Name of chord: C   Am   F   Dm   G7   C

Let's refer to these chords by the step of the scale upon which each chord is built. We'll use Roman numerals: large for major chords and small for minor chords. Between I and vi, you probably did not feel much increase in energy, but, if anything, a small reduction. From vi to IV, there is a slight increase, a small tug of tension. When we go to the ii chord, there is not an increase, but just an extension of the energy we have so far accumulated. When you go to the V7 chord, however, there is a big pull forward. Because of the dissonances within the chord, the pull for resolution is very strong. When you play the final chord, the I chord, the chord progression is resolved. Try playing this chord progression several times, with no dynamic shadings. You will soon become aware of the ability of dissonance in a harmonic progression to spur that progression forward.

If a rhythm is added to the above chord progression, the tension is heightened.

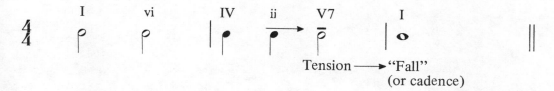

Tension ——▶ "Fall"
(or cadence)

This is the essence of harmonic rhythm. With every piece you play, be conscious of this rhythm. Allow it to shape your phrases, and work with your dynamics, so you can achieve a well balanced phrase structure.

PRACTICE POINTERS

Gavotta

1. The harmonic rhythm, marked by x's below the bass line, closely follows the motion of the bass voice. It is easy to see the rhythm quickening before the cadences. You can call attention to this in bars 3 and 7 by playing the bass notes more *staccato*.

2. For each beat (two per bar), block the notes so you can feel where the notes lie on the keyboard. Don't worry about the dissonances, that's part of the beauty of this piece.

3. Keep your dynamics between *p* and *mf*. This music was originally written for the harpsichord, and it didn't get a much larger dynamic range than that.

4. The bass should be warm and *legato* throughout. You should contrast this with a light, running sound in the right hand.

5. In the upbeats to the first and second bars, you should guide your playing with the shadow of the gavotte dance step. I have marked it in the music. This upbeat motive is found throughout, and should serve as a guide.

6. Keep your right-hand touch light. Drop your left hand onto each bass note with a slightly weighted *staccato* touch.

GAVOTTA

Arcangelo Corelli
(1658-1713)

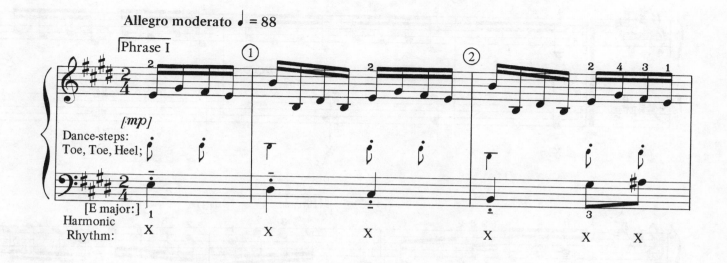

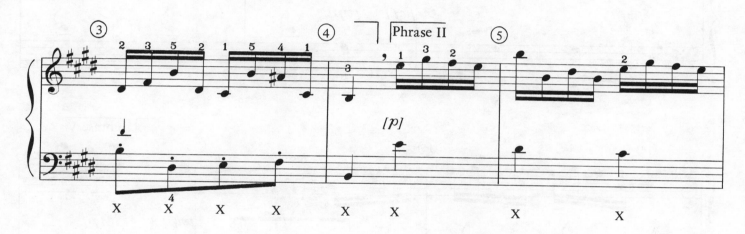

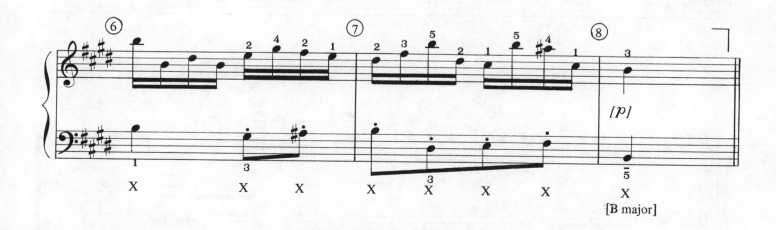

127

LARGHETTO

I. Stravinsky
(1882-1971)

Notice how the dissonance in this piece drives it onward.

With a gentle lilt

soloistic

on the f side

suddenly less loud

less f

with an even intensity

steadily onward

129

CHAPTER 20

KEY CHANGES (MODULATION)

Expressive playing should take into account any key changes which occur within a piece. Play the tonic scale of a piece you are working on. That scale will undoubtedly change several times over the course of the piece. These changes may be very brief promises of a key yet to come.

While discussing cadences, we saw that different chords bear different degrees of tension. The chord with the highest tension was the dominant (V7) chord, which led to the tonic (I) chord. These two chords belong together. Together they form the most common cadence.

When a composer wants to change keys, he must insert into the old scale tones which lead into the new scale. You can see where the composer does this, because suddenly the music will be peppered with one or more recurring accidentals which were not seen before.

Let's look at this example in C major.

Schumann: Little Humming Song, from Op. 68

> *Chromatic changes may be brief promises of a key yet to come.*

Notice in the third bar that there's an *F#*. This *F#* doesn't belong in C major, and the double bar before it makes me suspect something is happening. If you go farther into the piece, you will see three more *F#*'s in as many bars. By now, this *F#* has established itself in our ears as part of the scale of the piece. The *F#* is the note which leads us to the new key, and it is called a *leading tone*. The leading tone is always found on the seventh degree of the scale, just below the tonic note. Since this leading tone is an *F#*, we can say, therefore, that the new key we are in is the key of G. This ''accidental'' is no accident. A few bars later, we are given a full cadence in G major, confirming the key promised by the accidental. It seems only natural to me that, since *G* is a higher pitch than *C*, this cadence should be brighter and lighter than those before it. It should, at the very least, be expressed differently.

Schumann: Little Humming Song (cont'd)

Later in the piece, he returns the *F#* to its normal position of *F natural*, thereby returning the piece to the original key of C major.

All accidentals are interesting because of the color they bring to a piece of music. If they keep recurring, then it's a good bet that they are asserting a new scale in place of the old scale; we have been given a modulation (or key change). If the accidentals disappear, or are replaced by new ones, watch out! There's another new key around the corner. Every new accidental can lead to a new key. Whether it disappears before a new key can be established, or hangs around long enough to be confirmed, its effect on music is very important. No new accidental should be treated neutrally. Treat each one as the potential leading tone it often turns out to be.

PRACTICE POINTERS

Sonata

1. It is interesting to note that this piece was originally written in 3/8, not 3/4.

2. In measure 14, there is an *F#*. This, combined with the bass, forms a D7 chord which promises to go to G major. Remember, the *F#* is a *possible* leading tone. It has not yet been confirmed.

3. In measure 15, we are presented with an *E flat*. This darkens the C major chord to C minor, but doesn't change the key. A modal change, from major to minor, does not change the key you're in, just the mood.

4. In bar 16, the *F#* is repeated on a strong beat in a prominent range on the piano. It cannot be ignored, and it points more strongly to the key of G major.

5. In measure 20, the expected G major cadence happens. We are now in the key of G major.

6. In measure 21, the *E flat* of measure 15 is recalled, once again darkening the color of the C chord from major to minor.

7. If you block the notes of the right hand in measure 22, you will see that our *F#* has become *F natural* again. It makes this chord a G7 chord, and eliminates the leading tone. This is done in the middle of a harmonic sequence, and the composer slips it in so well, that we don't realize we are back in C major until the final cadence.

SONATA

Domenico Scarlatti
(1685-1757)

Heinrich Neuhaus, the famous Russian teacher of Emil Gilels and Sviatislav Richter would begin each lesson with dynamics. The student sat down and played a single note as softly as it could be heard. Then, the student would repeat the note, adding as many degrees of intensity as he could. Then, he or she would slowly get softer again, until the sound verged upon inaudible. Neuhaus was trying to get his students to keep from reaching the peak of sound too soon, and from losing sound too quickly during the diminuendo. The professor was not satisfied with less than ten degrees of increase or decrease, and would only begin to smile when a student reached *seventeen* shades either way.

It will be very difficult to reach seventeen dynamic levels, but you should start by having two levels between your *piano* and your *forte*. Take these five pitches in a row, playing each pitch at a slightly higher level.

Now, play the same five pitches in a descending pattern.

You can put them together in a little pattern with a flare at the end.

You can try playing the above "roulade" with level dynamics: all *p* or all *f*. You will notice that it lacks life and animation, though. This is not to say that rising pitches should always be accompanied by a crescendo, and all falling pitches by a decrescendo. You can create a wonderful effect by reversing that pattern.

Long range dynamic changes must be played with the subtlest degrees of *crescendo* or *decrescendo*, each note contributing to the change of intensity. Pianists often respond to the term *crescendo* with a sudden surge of intensity, causing them to reach the peak of the phrase too soon, ruining the rest of the phrase. Likewise, at the word *diminuendo,* many players get too soft too soon, making a mistake which cannot be corrected by the addition of another crescendo. Think of dynamics as the temperature of the music, with varying degrees of hot and cold.

In addition to a long, drawn out *crescendo* or *decrescendo*, a composer may ask for sudden changes in dynamic levels. You must play these very cleanly, and be sure that all the notes can be heard. They should not be smothered by the sudden change.

Think of dynamics as the temperature of the music, with varying degrees of hot and cold.

Schubert: Impromptu, A flat, Op. 142, no. 2

Dynamics cannot be separated from tone quality. A loud *staccato* tone pierces the ear more than a loud legato tone. That is because the *staccato* tone, being shorter, carries less string vibration, and more percussive hammer sound. If the notes should be separated, as with a *staccato* passage, the dynamics will hold them together as a unit.

Try singing the above example in a *legato* way. It seems natural to get louder as you go up, and get softer as you go down. This is because dynamics bring alive the feeling in music. They animate the action and reaction of the pitches. (If pitch is what the notes "do," then dynamics are how they "feel" about what they do.)

Let's look at the relationship between dynamic control and touch. When you were trying Professor Neuhaus' seventeen shades between *piano* and *forte,* where in the key were you playing? Play well into the key, right at the spot where the key begins to offer resistance. This is the spot where the hammer is triggered into motion. Too much "play" in the key action will give you poor results, extra noise and lost time.

Dynamics are also inseparable from tempo. It's a lot easier to create a clear dynamic shape at a moderate tempo than it is at a fast tempo.

136

Chopin: Valse ("Minute"), D flat, Op. 64, no. 1

Never sacrifice dynamic shape for speed. All you will be able to express is your ability to play fast. Listen to the expressive loss as you increase speed (but not intensity) in this example.

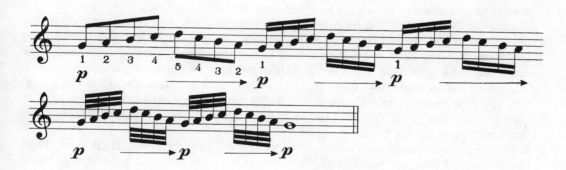

All you have is an expressively neutral hum. There are instances where this is a required part of the music, as in the Waldstein Sonata by Beethoven below.

Allegro con brio

Beethoven: Allegro con brio, Sonata ("Waldstein"), C, Op. 53

Do not let this "hum" happen by accident. Dynamics and tempo are the only tools a pianist has to express himself or herself. Lack of dynamics are very often the reason people leave a recital saying "It was all notes; it left me cold."

Here is a list of some dynamic points to be aware of:

1. If a composer marks a dynamic level, you should maintain that level until the next marking. This may be many bars away, so be very conscious of the level you are playing.

2. If the composer has not marked any dynamic fluctuations (such as *crescendi* and *decrescendi,* this does not mean that you should play deadpan. Always add nuances to a piece of music.

3. In an *Urtext* (original text) edition, the composer's original markings are printed in bold face. The editor's additional markings are a lighter typeface, or are set apart by the use of brackets. Unfortunately, these editions were not around before 1945, so it is impossible to tell which markings belong to whom in music printed before 1945.

4. You need not begin a *crescendo* or *decrescendo* as soon as you see the marking. The majority of such long term changes should happen toward the end of the span of the change.

5. The difference between *piano* and *forte* markings is very great. There should be a noticeable difference in the energy level between these two markings.

6. Let your dynamic extremes be guided by the instrument, the hall you are playing in, the number of people present, etc. If you exceed the "full, round tone" recommended by C.P.E. Bach, you inherit noises such as keys hitting the keybed, hammer noise, and other unwanted noises. All these noises are magnified by the sounding board and piano case.

7. *Forte* tones are dependent upon the speed with which the hammer strikes the string, which, in turn, depends upon the speed with which your finger hits the key. You can awaken your *fortes* by using the "speed" muscles inside your palm, rather than depending upon dropped arm weight for tone production.

8. Players often shy at the term *piano*, losing the focus of their tone production. It's too bad that we refer to them as "soft" tones. They should be just as clear and bell-like as our loud tones.

9. Apply some dynamic shading to every note group, no matter how small. Two slurred notes should either sigh $\diagdown$ or surge $\diagup$, but they should never remain the same. Mozart told us to "give expression to each note," and we must try to follow his wishes.

10. In the film "Casablanca," Humphrey Bogart uttered the famous line "Play it again, Sam, with feeling." This was his call for dynamic shading. For every piece you play, draw a dynamic "fever chart," showing the basic dynamic structure of the piece. It should look something like this:

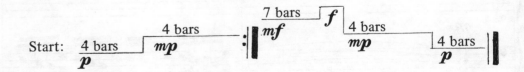

PRACTICE POINTERS

Theme from Etude, Op. 10, No. 3

1. This edition is a composite of most of Chopin's known markings for what he once called his ''most perfect melody.''

2. The melody will either sink or swim, depending on the dynamic shadings given to it. Let it soar above the other accompaniment notes of the right and left hands.

3.The bass notes must support the melody on every new beat. They must be played with the melody, because they generate overtones which, in turn, further support the melody.

4. Use the dynamic levels given at the upbeat to the first measure as a guide to the prominence of each voice.

5. Be aware of the accent of the second note of the bass pattern in bars one and two. This note should be stressed, but not thumped.

6. There are three phrases in this excerpt. The first is five bars long, the second is three bars, and the third is five bars. Find the location of the heart of each phrase and mark it clearly in your music.

7. Chopin's *ma non troppo* (not too much) marking is reflected in the metronome marking. This tempo allows the long melodic lines to hang together. It is unhurried enough to clarify the levels of movement which coexist in the sonority, much like a string quartet.

8. You will notice that Chopin uses one dynamic marking. However, his nuance markings, together with the melody's ascension and descent, guide the dynamic levels within the piece.

ETUDE, E MAJOR
(THEME ONLY)
OP. 10, NO. 3

Frédéric Chopin
(1810-1849)

nce a pianist becomes bolder and more colorful through the use of dynamics, it's time to use dynamics to create dimension. It's time to separate the foreground from the background. First, let's discuss how to balance piano ranges.

Balance of Piano Ranges

The problem that often arises is the need to balance a fairly high melody against the deeper tones of the supporting harmonies and bass tones.

Satie: *Gymnopédie,* no. 3

Chopin: Nocturne, Eb major, Op. 9, no. 2

Chopin's *espressivo dolce* marking asks you to favor the melody over the rest of the texture. It should soar over the deep bass tones. The dots over the bass tones are Chopin's own markings. They do not indicate a staccato touch, but rather the opposite. They should be full, but distinctly separate from the accompanying chords. You can produce the necessary sound by using the full weight of your arm. You need the deep bass tones, not only to announce each new harmony, but to generate the overtones which enrich the melody. Chopin knew of this overtone principle, and deliberately placed his melodies in a range he knew would benefit them most.

Accompaniment figures do not always have to be suppressed. Their motion always suggests a mood or manner of movement, like an undulation. Notice how the change in the movement of the inner voices adds a subtle agitation to the second appearance of the theme.

Original appearance:

It's time to separate the foreground from the background.

Return later:

Beethoven: Adagio Cantabile, Sonata ("Pathétique"), C minor, Op. 13

You need to be very careful when separating a melody from an accompaniment which is only a few notes below.

Schumann: *The Joyous Farmer*, Op. 86, no. 10

In this situation, you must give the melody about twice the intensity of the accompaniment, or it will be disrupted and broken.

Melody tones which are part of the accompaniment harmony must be extremely prominent.

142

Mendelssohn: Song Without Words, E major, Op. 19, no. 1

This is especially important when the accompanying chords are repeated. The melody must be given enough life of its own to rise above the accompaniment.

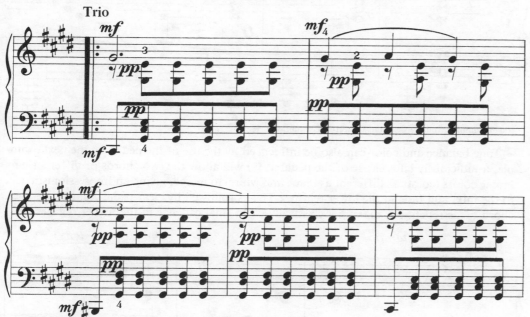

Schubert: Impromptu, A flat, Op. 90, no. 4 (D. 899)

Voicing Chords

The next topic we must discuss is voicing. The way a pianist highlights a particular note can contribute much to his tone color. A chord voice should stand out if:

1. It is the root of the chord (especially if it is in the bass).
2. It is the major or minor third of the chord; the pitch that gives a chord its mood.
3. It is the seventh of a dominant seventh chord.
4. It is a dissonant tone: not a chord tone, but a color tone.
5. It is a chromatic alteration added to any chord tone. This introduces directional tension (sharped notes tend to want to go up another half step to a chord tone, and flats want to go down.

I don't expect anyone to memorize all these instances, nor do I want to interrupt your enjoyment of chord colors by making you thoroughly confused. Composers are always writing chords that cannot be named. We must just listen to the degree of dissonant tension in the chord. Dissonance in music complicates harmony, challenging it until another chord triumphs over the dissonance, and the tension resolves. The example below, by Rachmaninoff, is a crystal clear example of prolonged dissonance eventually resolving to a consonance. His poetic brooding on dissonance, and the chaining of these dissonant pressures within repeated tolling tones, releases the "pain" of that dissonance into the relative "freedom" of consonance at the *a tempo*.

Rachmaninoff: Moderato, Second Concerto, C minor, Op. 18

Tone balance and color can also be influenced by the use of the pedal. In the next example, a judiciously late release of the pedal at (*) will allow the two chords of different harmonic colors (colors as different as black and white) to merge, giving an Impressionistic feel to the mix, and fade in the lower register. This is followed by clear pedal changes for each chord of its repetition, making a classically clean final cadence in the higher register.

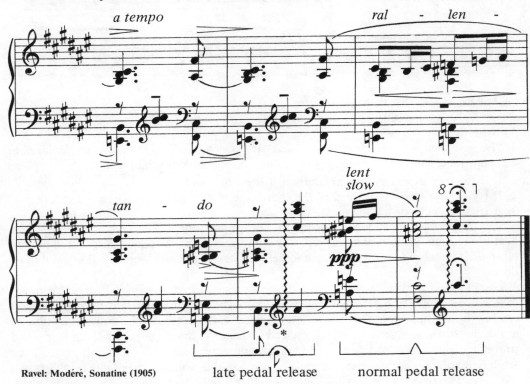

Ravel: Modéré, Sonatine (1905)

late pedal release   normal pedal release

Often, a composer will draw one tone from a haze, holding it up for your attention. A little pedal is desirable, so that, when the pedal is released, the C appears from nowhere.

"surface" pedal

144

late

pedal release

Chopin: Fourth Ballade, F minor, Op. 52

I call this technique cadence-by-focus. It is not a cadence as we discussed earlier, but rather, a technique used to add more color and texture to a piece. Here's another example.

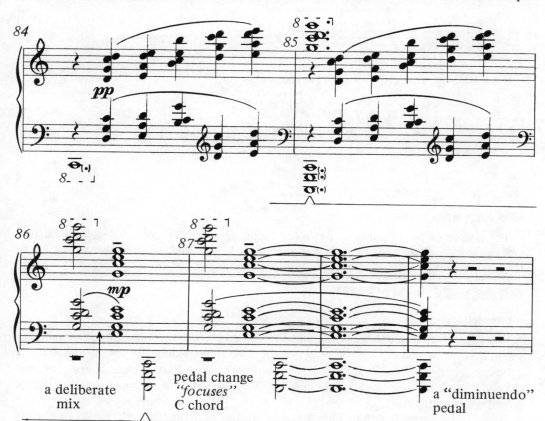

Debussy: *The Engulfed Cathedral* **(ending)**

Since the damper pedal is held from bar 85 to the end, an "acoustic cadence" occurs. This, too, is a coloration device used by composers. The last *D's* (bar 87) will fade first (dissonance usually is first to leave the listener's ear), leaving the consonant C chord free to emerge from the mist. This is quite like the cinematic technique of focusing a camera, but instead you are taking a blurred sound, and bringing it into focus.

The Balance of Sonority (or "Through Thick and Thin")

The thickness of sound present at any given moment is cause for concern for pianists. In our first example, Schumann begins with a thin solo line and a small "teardrop" of sound, adding even more voices as he goes on.

Nicht schnell (not fast)

Midway, more voices, streaming:

Ending, still more, with vehemence:

Schumann: *First Loss,* Op. 68, no. 16

The texture of the sound must be voiced by the pianist. The solo lines must be intense, and the thicker areas must be full of warm tones. You should use selective voicing in the thicker areas.

PRACTICE POINTERS

Solfeggietto

Note: This piece travels through the piano's full range, and alternates thick and thin textures. It is one of the most enduringly popular pieces ever written for the piano.

1. Notice that the only original dynamics are *forte* and *piano.* Make a clear contrast between the two, both in intensity and in character. The *fortes* should be bold, and the *pianos* should be animated and glittery.

2. While you are working on making the tempo faster, keep the sixteenths steady by slightly accenting each beat. This will also help you when it comes to adding dynamic shadings.

3. The dotted brackets do not mean that you should slur your touch. The proper touch for this piece is light, dry and clear (but not staccato).

4. When you add dynamic nuances, pencil them in until you are sure of them.

5. Remember to maintain C.P.E. Bach's dynamic levels until you encounter a new one.

6. The entire piece is a good example of the use of dynamics as an aid to phrasing. Phrasing must be extra clear when the notes are speeding by the ear, so that they will have direction. The shape of the phrases directly affects the speed with which you can play it. With well shaped phrases and dynamic nuances, this piece can sound very exciting at an *Allegro molto, Prestissimo,* even where possible, is perhaps less desirable. After all, *solfegietto* means "in the style of an Italian vocal exercise." For years, Italian opera singers were trained to sing like this.

146

SOLFEGGIETTO IN C MINOR
(WQ. 117/2)

Carl Philipp Emanuel Bach
(1714-1788)

3 tempos for study:
① Your first tempo = Allegro, mm ♩ = 116-120
② Then, Allegro molto, mm ♩ = 132
③ Later,

[sopra]
[Left hand *above* right hand]

[sopra]
[Left hand *above* right hand]

(Think)

(Think)

148

CHAPTER 23

FINGER PAINTING

 he brush stroke of a good painter is swift and sure. As you watch him work on this dot or that line, the smudges of color first hint at, then become, the whole picture - the big, detailed vision the artist has been seeing in his "mind's eye."

A good pianist is guided in the same way by the "mind's ear." Experience and emotion both add colors to plain pitches. Personal chemistry continually produces new mixes of these colors, and drives the pianist to seek new technical gestures that can "paint" them into the piano. His palette of touches often allows his playing to be identified.

Here is a survey of "brush strokes" you'll need.

Preparing to Paint

In order to shape the quality of sound we produce, we must become conscious of the exact spot where the piano tone is produced. That point in the key action lies nearly halfway into its descent. Officially, it's called the *escapement* (after the little jack that "kicks" the hammer inside). I call it the *tone-spot*. You can find it quickly on a grand piano. Just press one key down slowly until you meet a slight resistance midway. Think of your finger as actually touching the hammer there, and "pop" it toward the string.

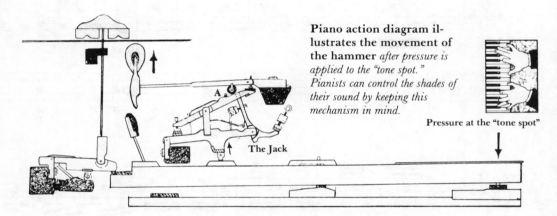

Piano action diagram illustrates the movement of the hammer *after pressure is applied to the "tone spot." Pianists can control the shades of their sound by keeping this mechanism in mind.*

Pressure at the "tone spot"

A

The Jack

That small nudge conveys immediate energy to A, the leathered knuckle under the long end of the hammer shank. Increasing finger pressure causes the jack underneath that knuckle to send the hammer the rest of the way up toward the string. The action is like bunting a baseball from the bat.

This energy contact is so immediate that *the speed and timing of the hammer blow matter much more than force.* A hammer popped quickly produces a louder, brighter sound, while a more deliberate pressure at the tone-spot gives a mellow, large, carrying sound. The tone-spot is the pianist's bow and the hammer is his arrow.

Legato Touch: Sound Melting into Sound

Let's begin our survey of "brush strokes" with *legato,* a smooth connection of notes. Though *legato* is an illusion, made possible by cleverly minimizing hammer strokes in favor of string sounds, it is also the trademark of a pianist's success. In Paris in 1978, I questioned Lionel de Pachmann about how his legendary father, Vladimir (1848-1933), had gotten his marvelous melting of tones that still sings in historical recordings. In answer, Lionel sat down, at age ninety-two, and played this excerpt from Chopin's Nocturne in E flat, Op. 9, No.2:

There it was, the famous melting merger of tones *"sans marteaux"* (without hammers)! He held the keys deep, and repeated or connected tones without letting them up. There was some changing of fingers for repetitions. There was certainly a full tone for each note, and a sense that it grew from, and replaced the previous one. (Note his dynamics!)

Part of the illusion consists of that full, warm tone that overlays and disguises the initial hammer blow of the next tone. Part of it also lies in riding the key "low in the saddle," so that no key ever has far to travel toward its strings. Try this exercise with a light surge toward the *second* note of each two note slur; minute dynamic gradings allow the ear to "seal" the gaps from note to note.

2 - note links to a legato line:

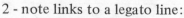

151

To sustain this illusion, one must also watch tapering intensities, especially the marked decay of a long tone. Match the hammer blow of the new tone with what is left of the long one.

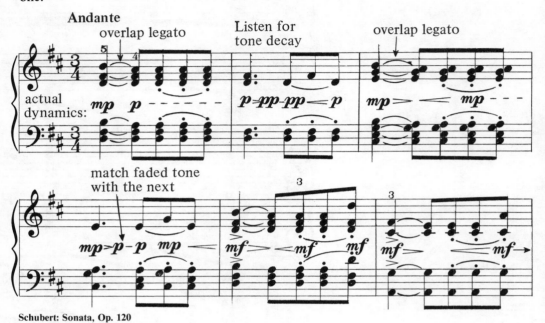

Schubert: Sonata, Op. 120

Since touch, like taste and sight, can be stimulated by its opposite, light *staccato* taps will seem like a "smoothing" of your brush before its next lush stroke.

In the example below, the high register demands extra intensities to maintain a sense of line:

Beethoven: Sonata ("Pathétique"), C minor, Op. 13

Staccato

Return now to the tone-spot - the pressure point where a minute impulse of the fingertip "pops" the hammer to the string. Though the hammer rebounds immediately from its blow on the string (which allows you to repeat the note without raising the key), the depressed key still holds up the damper (or the sound could not continue).

To cut off the sound, you need only raise the key from the tone-spot to the point where the sinking damper stops the vibrating strings. This is an *infinitesimal* rise of the key. This basic *staccato,* in which you decide where the sound stops, I call a "contact *staccato.*" As with *legato* touch, minimizing energy and movement at the tone-spot will consciously refine the point where you cut off the sound and let in the silence. Try allowing one part sound to one part silence, like this:

At A, pop the key right at the tone spot;

at B, let the key rebound naturally, but *only* to the point where the damper snuffs the sound.

Play:

Incidentally, did you notice that the damper did not stop the string sound immediately, but by gradually shading its vibrations? Each alteration of the vibratory pattern will change its tone color and awaken some of the harmonics of the strings. This is a rich color resource for slow fadeouts.

The following chart will help you to place some of the most common touches on a *legato-staccato* continuum.

Legatissimo (Overlap Legato)

Extra holding "melts" one tone into another:

Mozart, *Fantasy* in D minor K.397

By not lifting each tone, Brahms arrives at a total "overlap":

Brahms, *Intermezzo* in B minor, Op. 119 no. 1

Normal Legato
Legato uses a warm tone to conceal the hammer blow of the tone which follows.

Slurred Legato

One tone is stressed, the other is noticeably lighter.

Schubert, *Moment Musicale* in A Flat Op. 96 no. 6

In a rapid tempo the stress stands out.

Beethoven, *Sonata* Op. 13 (Pathétique)

Non Legato (Only Slightly Disconnected)

Bach, *Menuet* from French Suite III

Portato (Similar To Portamento For The Voice)

The hand weight is "dragged" from note to note; the sound leans toward *legato,* but with a heavier, expressive touch.

Grieg, *Arietta* Op. 12 no. 1

Staccato-Tenuto (Long Staccato)

The sound lingers past the midbeat, and is played without hand weight.

Chopin's bass staccato dots (as below) often mean this touch, without an accent.

Chopin, *Nocturne* in G minor Op. 15 no. 3

Normal Staccato

Mozart uses notation to convey normal staccato in the example below.

Mozart, *Concerto* in C Major K.467

Short Staccato

Beethoven, *Sonata* in F minor Op. 2 no. 1

Staccatissimo (The Shortest Staccato; Often Louder)

The shorter the sound, the brighter the "pop" of the hammer. Debussy's "quasi guitarra" draws on a whole rainbow of plucked sounds.

Debussy, *La sérénade interrompue* from Preludes, book I

Now I would like to share some of the images I use to help animate the hand as it "paints" those tonal shades and landscapes.

On The Legato Side

For warm, *legato* sounds, "squeeze the juice from every key;" or "press your fingerprint" into the ivory.

For an active hand-shaping of a small group of notes, "lean into the wind as you go."

Mozart: Fantasy (K. 475)

Focusing A Tone

The ear can be drawn to a single sounding tone by elimination. A full, pedaled sonority is "sheared away" by levels of pedal and hand weight until only one tone still sounds, which seems to *crescendo*.

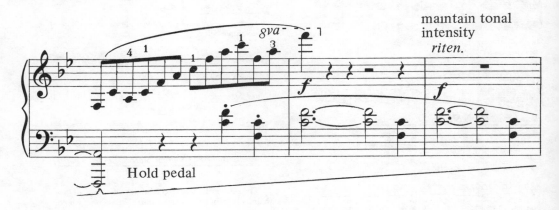

Chopin: First Ballade, G minor, Op. 23

Focusing happens at
pedal release

Put An Ear-Ring Into Your Ornament

Accent the sound of the main note (the starting note) of a trill, turn or mordent. It is the continuing vibration of the initial tone that "ornaments" or adds luster to the melody.

"Ring" the *initial* tone

Glistening Glissandi

Begin your glissando rather slowly, then trail your arm weight in a single sweeping stroke as you continue.

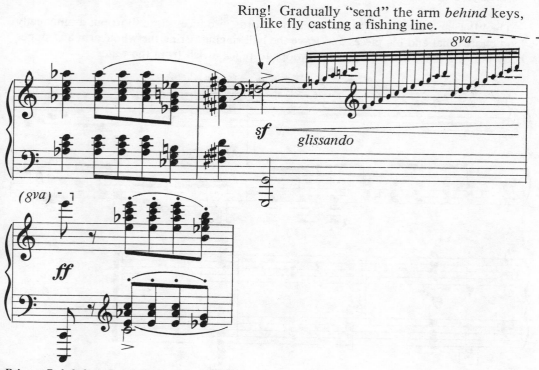

Ring! Gradually "send" the arm *behind* keys, like fly casting a fishing line.

Debussy: Prelude from *Pour le Piano*

On The Staccato Side

"Salt and pepper" or "perforated line" staccato is achieved through legato fingering, lightly "flicked" to the tone-spot.

Bach: Two-Part Invention No. 13

"Needlepoint" staccato swiftly pricks the skin of the keys.

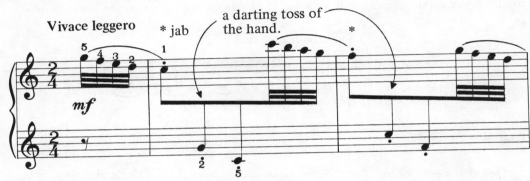

Kabalevsky: *A Little Joke*

light needle pricks

The "Pelican Plunge" touch, for concerto chords, produces those short but dramatically loud chords that end big pieces and leave the hall ringing. Bring the whole arm and upper body into the tone, just as a pelican swoops to pluck a fish from the water.

Beethoven: Sonata ("Waldstein"), C, Op. 53

Equally suggestive as images are those of other instruments of the orchestra. I was able to quiet some pianistic chatter the other day with this orchestral scenario:

Mozart: Sonata (K. 309)

PRACTICE POINTERS

Arioso and Burlesca

Here's a chance to develop two contrasting touches that often are used in good piano playing.

Arioso

Bars 1-8: This slow introduction to the *Burlesca* calls for the *portato* touch in the left hand. Much misunderstood, this is a touch that pianists often need for deliberate expressiveness. The misunderstanding lies, in part, from the awkward appearance of the dots-under slurs, *portato* symbol:

Acting upon well-drilled impulse, most pianists take their hands *off* the keys in uncertain degrees of *staccato*. The true touch is rather the opposite. The hand must hang heavily *into* the key, *preventing* its rise and a break in the sound before its repetition.

Let the hand hang loosely *down into* the key action, and let its released weight simply carry over or drag from one key to its repetition, or to the next key. *Portato* in Italian means "carried," while the equivalent in German usage is *getragen* — literally, "dragged."

Think of your hand as a cork floating in water. It neither sinks to the bottom, nor jumps out of the water. It just floats with the key action at the point where the tone may be repeated.

The following little prep will help you "test the water," and get the feel of your own key action:

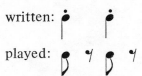 *(Continue up C scale)*

Since you are "treading water," don't let your hand sink to the keybed. Rather, let it dangle from a slightly raised wrist until it locates the spot (about 3/8 inch) down *into* the key descent where the sound may be repeated. Those repetitions should "vibrate" on that spot.

The right hand needs a full *mf* for every note, especially the shorter values. It plays *mf* to the *mp* of the *left hand* as if the soaring line of a solo violin were being set off by the muted accompaniment of celli and violas.

Repeat the entire *Arioso* with respectively softer dynamic levels.

Burlesca

Bars 1-12: Everywhere you have the simple dot above a note (𝅘𝅥) you have the normal *staccato* touch, which needs about *half the value* of given note. So, in the first two bars and other places, the right hand should play an eighth note, followed by an eighth rest, for the quarter notes:

written:

played:

Bar 3: The staccato eighth notes, then, would be played as sixteenths, each followed by a sixteenth rest:

The only difference is that notes *on* the beat should be played with more energy than those on the *off*-beat. In addition, a lively piece like this calls for slightly more stress on the downbeat of beat one. So, press *into* the first note of each bar firmly: this touch is called *staccato-tenuto*.

ARIOSO

Georg Philipp Telemann
(1681-1767)

(go on to Burlesca
without a break)

BURLESCA

Georg Philipp Telemann
(1681-1767)

CHAPTER 24

SILENCES — THE "REST-LESS 'REST'"

Music is born from silence, and silences, mixed with sounds, are anything but "dead" silences. In fact, the planned silences in music (rests) speak volumes!

Imagine that you are alone at midnight in a large house. Suddenly, you hear a soft knock at the back door. You stop, inhale and wait. Was that a knock? Or did you imagine it? You decide it's nothing and resume your reading. Again you hear a knock. There's no mistake, there's someone or something there.

Was the silence between the time that you heard the first knock and you resumed your reading a restful silence? Hardly! It had you frozen, on red alert. It is precisely this "midnight silence," suspenseful, full of expectation that the pianist hopes to create when he strides on stage, sits, and raises his hands. The pianist draws on this highly charged focus of attention. It is echoed in the rests throughout a piece, and, if he has used the energy well, it echoes in the silence following the last rest.

Poet John Keats said "Sounds unheard are sweeter still." Let's explore the meaning of this, because sound and silence are the mediums that every musician works with.

Musicians rely on silences to punctuate sounds in the same way that orators rely on pauses to punctuate speech. The degree of stress felt in musical silences matters as much for the meaning of the music as does the degree of stress felt in musical sound. As an example, listen to the silence at (*) in Beethoven's Sonata Pathetique.

"Sounds unheard are sweeter still."

The questioning or searching effect of the silence is due to the full booming sound of the opening chord. This is a cause and effect relationship. What makes that opening chord boom? It is what the pianist heard in the silence before the first chord, before he lifted his hands to play. A good musician will think through the beats of a full bar of silence in tempo, with a slight crescendo of intensity, as if to collect and compact the silence for the next measure. This will help the listeners be surprised by the opening chord. No silence in music is without energy, and if this thought is projected by the pianist, then the music will be charged with that energy.

How, then, may we electrify each rest in order to punctuate an idea in progress, or to cool the ear before something new happens? Consider the following ways in which we use silence.

Just as music comes from silence, so must it return to silence. Many composers want their music to stop dead in its tracks, as seen in this example by Chopin.

Chopin: Valse, E minor, Op. 72 (posthumous), end

Other composers allow their music to sink into the silence, much like a submarine sinks under the surface of the water.

Chopin: Prelude, E minor, Op. 28, no. 4, end

In this example, Chopin defies the inevitable silence by using a modulation sequence, crescendo, and recurring B (which is the fifth, not the root of the final chord).

Chopin: Prelude, E major, No. 9

The trick here is to crescendo very late (to give the impression that there's more to come), and lift both hands and the pedal after the final chord has been heard, but before it begins to die away. This emphasizes Chopin's defiance of silence.

A composer will often give you more rests than notes at the end of a piece, extending the end of the piece with seemingly unstoppable rhythm. The fermata over the last rest creates the most active rest you will encounter.

Beethoven: end of first movm't., Sonata ("Pathétique"), C minor, Op. 13

A sudden cutoff can have a humorous effect, as in this piece by Haydn.

Haydn: Presto (finale), Sonata, A flat (Hob. XVI/46)

A true speaking silence is a clever illusion that convinces you that the music is still being heard. A vital sound awakens a vital rest. If you look at the sun, then put your hands over your eyes, you will see a black negative impression of the sun. It is a similar negative impression of a vivid sound which causes a silence to ring.

From the fairly strong silences we have looked at, let's go on and examine some low key silences that articulate musical speech. Let's start by looking at offbeat rests which subtly push along a piece.

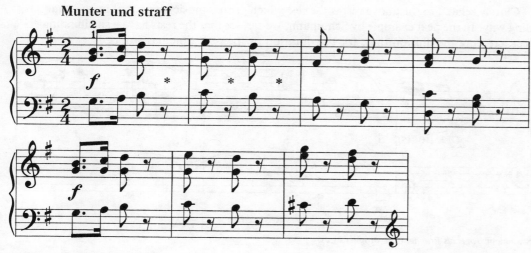

Munter und straff

Schumann: Soldier's March, Op. 68

Then there are rests which are supercharged, and do not "march," as did the above example, but "dance" instead.

Chopin: Ballade, A flat, Op. 47, no. 3, opening

Closely related to the above rest is the rest which pushes music along, but in a very unsettling way. In the next example by Schumann, we can see that the rests have a spellbinding effect, creating the illusion that, for the duration of the rest, time has stopped.

Schumann: *Vogel als Prophet* **(The Prophet Bird)**

Let us not forget the tiny pinpricks of silence which separate quick notes, or group many notes together for better musical sense (this often happens in music of the Baroque era).

Rameau: Menuet, from Pièces de clavecin

These tiny points of silence are often used to sharpen an accented note (as in a staccato note).

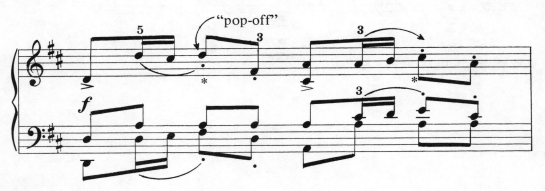

Pachelbel: Canon in D

There are many other uses for rests. Some are funny, some are shocking, some are small and many are large. Whatever their size, the effect that they have is primarily due to their placement among the beats in a measure. Play the Schubert Impromptu below several times.

Schubert: Impromptu, A flat, Op. 90, no. 4 (D. 899)

Then, insert a rest in the left hand for the third beat, like this:

The rest will sound very light, because it occurs on a weak beat. If the composer puts the rest on a strong beat, the effect is very different.

Schumann: Waltz, A minor, Op. 124, no. 4

The rest will sound very strong (depending on how clean the cutoff from the previous note). If this "clean cut" rest comes prematurely, the effect can be quite funny.

J. Strauss, Jr.: Tritsch-Tratsch Polka, Op. 214

There is really no end to what these non-silent rests can say. Many musicians spend their lifetimes trying to achieve this or that inflection. It is never enough to merely register a rest. You must play it with the exact degree of punctuation, surprise, sigh, or breath that is necessary to help dramatize your musical narrative.

PRACTICE POINTERS

Arabesque from Op. 100

Bars 1 and 2: Place your hand on the A minor bass chord. You can suggest Near-Eastern mystery with a quick, dry surface "rap" touch, short enough to leave plenty of silence between each sound:

Bars 3-6: This subtle, but startling secret pause is expanded into the sudden question that punctuates each sixteenth note spurt via the rest at the end of each of these bars.

To make that sudden silence "speak," treat the dot at the end of the slur at beat two as an *accented* staccato:

Bars 11-16: Transfer that same clear articulation to the left hand here. At the same time, play the right hand with a full *legato* tone (on short notes especially). The right hand is *mf* over *mp* in the left.

Bars 17-18: Play especially *legato* here, giving the left hand a slight edge over the right, despite the general *diminuendo*. It must *roll* right into the returning theme at Bar 19.

Bars 19-22: The opening theme returns, with its mysterious dry drumbeat (*all* those left-hand chords are staccato throughout the piece).

Continue the *crescendo* right *through* the interrupted second beat of Bar 22.

Bars 23-26: Don't be afraid to rub in that "true grit" dissonance in the bass chords here. Change fingers for the sparky upbeat in the right hand:

Bars 26-31: Play the bass D minor chords stronger than the A minor ones, within a general *crescendo* to Bar 30. At Bar 30, mark your "resolution" *(risoluto)* at the *e* to *a* fifth of the little run, and don't rush your sixteenth notes!

Bar 31: Press the pedal down *before* you play the last chord, then hold it *through* the second beat for a clean lift.

ARABESQUE
FROM OP. 100

J.F.F. Bürgmüller
(1806-1874)

Many of the pieces you play on the piano began as simple melodies. They may be transcribed from songs, operatic arias, symphonies, or concertos. They have been arranged for the piano with broken chords to suggest harps or clarinets. As poor as some of these arrangements may be, people buy them in thick volumes because they make a wide range of music accessible to the pianist. They contradict the notion that the piano, a percussion instrument, cannot successfully reproduce melodies that were intended for the voice or violin.

This is a very touchy point. Pianists devote their lives to the illusion that good full tones, dynamically shaped, can imitate the flowing *legato* lines that a singing melody requires. In order to "sing" on the piano, you need to melt one tone into the next, and then the next, creating a seamless line of sound. Try this exercise for linking seconds together.

This is a very touchy point.

"The creepy-crawlie's" — *links* to a *legato* line:

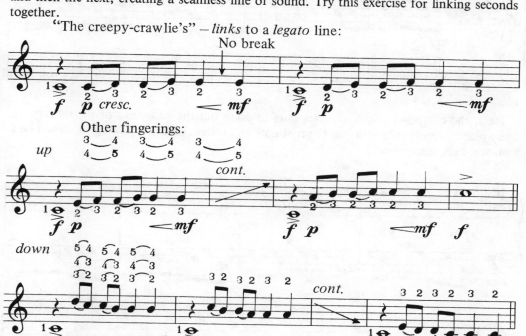

After you have mastered the seconds, try to melt together tones of gradually widening and contracting intervals.

When you can play this exercise in several keys with your eyes shut, you can rest assured that you are beginning to soak in the sound and feel of common melodic intervals. In order to become familiar with the less common intervals (those which strongly express feeling through chromatic coloration), work the same pattern through all twelve intervals of the chromatic scale.

Working on these exercises, one per day, will help you go far towards creating the singing "voice" and line of your melodies. Don't be shy! If you are faced with a melody, play it out!

Let's begin to look at some examples of these legato intervals. In the first, C.P.E. Bach places a slur marking only where he wants an important interval connected and stressed.

C.P.E. Bach: Rondo in B minor

Here, the composer selectively uses slurs to point out the vital links of the melody. In these places, you should lean into the first note and release on the following (it should be a lean-and-light connection).

Schubert: Allegretto, Sonata, G, Op. 78 (D. 894)

If the melody you are faced with is over an octave above middle C, you should play it at least one dynamic level above the accompaniment so it will not seem "high and dry."

MacDowell: *To A Wild Rose*, Op. 51, no. 1

172

If your melody has a strong dissonance in it, lean into the dissonance. This will help it be independent of the harmony.

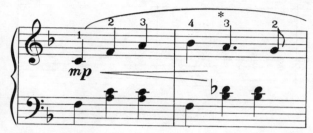

Tchaikovsky: Waltz of the Flowers

Now that we have seen some examples of melody, let's talk about how to play them. Here are some points that will improve the tone quality, shape and articulation of your melodic voice.

1. Link every interval, especially the wider intervals, so that the ear registers a leap, but not a break, in the melody.

Link, (even "overlap")
this 6th.

Liszt: *Liebestraum*

2. Start every phrase clearly, especially if it begins with an upbeat after a rest.

Mozart: Allegro, Sonata, G. (K. 283)

3. Give every phrase clear direction. Be sure to give it a start, a heart and an end.

Mozart: Allegro, Sonata, F. (K. 332)

4. Supply your longer melody tones with greater intensity. Make sure, though, that they are connected to the following shorter tones. The shorter notes should come out of the sound of the longer notes, and should not accidentally start a new idea.

Clementi: Allegro con spirito, Sonatina, D, Op. 36, no. 6

5. Look for the hidden scales that structure melody and give it both direction and suspense.

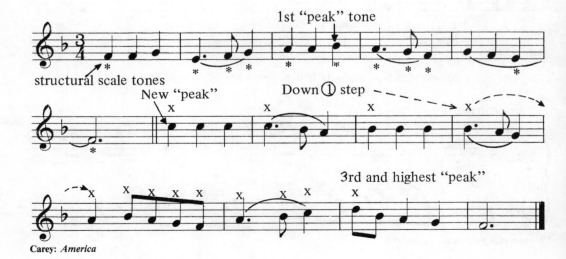

Carey: America

6. Use dynamics to give your scales direction. Like a staircase, these scales lead somewhere.

Händel: Courante, F

7. Repeated notes must also show direction. They should either grow toward a goal, or fade away from one. This is done by skillfully using dynamics.

Poco Andante e sostenuto

Grieg: Arietta, Op. 12, no. 1

175

8. Begin every *crescendo* as late as possible, but carry it through to its goal. Don't let it fizzle out.

Brahms: Rhapsody, G minor, Op. 79, no. 2

9. Shape your contour notes, that is, the notes just before, during, and after a change in melodic direction. You can easily lose your listener "around the bend."

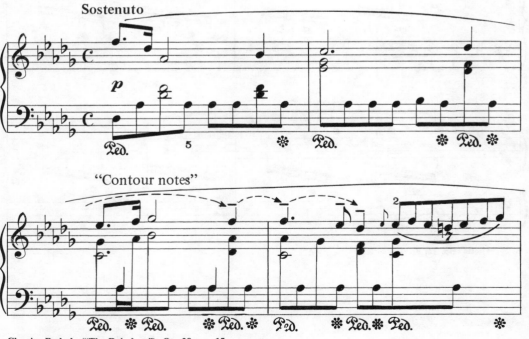

Chopin: Prelude ("The Raindrop"), Op. 28, no. 15

10. Make sure that melodic cadences are emphasized. Often they consist of a two-note slur, where the first note is dissonant and stressed, and the second is relaxed, and disappears like a sigh.

Mozart: Andante, Sonata, C (K. 545)

11. Don't rush, blur or dim the quality of the smaller melodic notes. This can be as fatal to your melody as mumbling would be to a speech. These small notes also are part of the lyrical meaning of a melody. Every note must be allowed to sing out.

Schubert: Andante, Sonata, A, Op. 120 (D. 664)

12. Press into the keys where the melody note is dissonant. The "pain" of the dissonance strongly urges the melody onward.

Mozart: Fantasy, C minor (K. 475)

PRACTICE POINTERS

Andantino

1. The background begins first in the left hand. The touch should be tenuto, and the repeating quarter notes should cling together. Try to play them right on the tone-spot of the key, about a third of the way down in its descent, without letting the key rise to its full height.

2. The right hand melody is derived from the C natural minor scale (save the A natural of bar 25). The left hand descends by the half steps of the chromatic scale. Play the two scales alongside each other, and you will sense the dynamic contrast they make; the left hand pulling downward, while the right hand "holds the line."

Right: descending the C natural-minor scale.

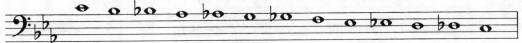

Left: descending the *chromatic* scale (by half-steps).

3. Be sure that the syncopation of the left hand is lively from bar 18 to the end. You should think steady eighths from bar 17 on. This will help the transition from quarters to the syncopated eighth/quarter pattern. Make the first note of each syncopated pair slightly louder than the second.

(L.H. plays)

4. Throughout the piece, the right hand has a level, sincere quality. Be careful not to rush the eighths.

178

ANDANTINO

Aram Khachaturian
(1903-1978)

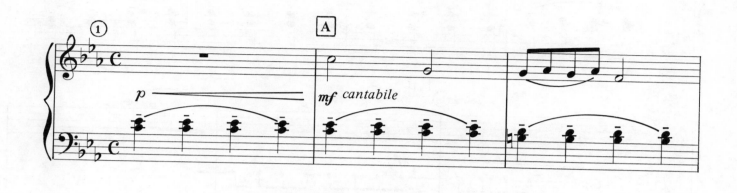

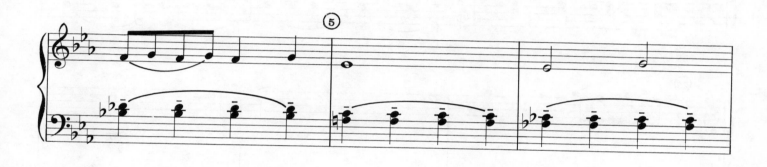

CHAPTER 26

A WORD ON ORNAMENTS

All of us are a little frightened by what we do not know, and many players just leave out the little signs that are encrusted all over Bach's music, and that are occasionally seen in Chopin's music. They have survived through centuries of rich improvisation. For the improviser of long ago, ornamental notes were a way to accent a note, or fill in the gap between many notes. Many of these practices are still evident in the music we play today. They are called *appoggiaturas,* and are seen in ordinary notation (not those little notes).

Schubert: *Moments Musicaux,* A flat, Op. 94, no. 6 (D. 780)

Many ornaments continue their ancient life as signs such as ᴡ , ∾ , and ᴡ . These signs give us only a general indication of what we are to do. How are we to play them? Are they always the same? A complete answer to these questions would take an entire book, and many have been devoted to just that. You might want to begin with a small, but very practical book entitled "Keyboard Interpretation," by Howard Ferguson (Oxford University Press, 1975).

You see, in Bach's and Mozart's time, notes which were written smaller than the regular notes were the *important* ones. They were written smaller to catch the eye, not to dodge it. That is why nearly all of these ornaments are played *on* the beat, and are often dissonant with the supporting harmony. An ornamental tone is almost never separated from the resolution; they should melt together. Even if a slur is not written over them, the player should think of them as slurred.

How are we to play those ancient signs?

J.S. Bach: Minuet, G. (from "Anna Magdalena Little Book")

Personally, I prefer the melodic independence of a quicker resolution in the right hand (b). I would recommend that you play both versions and decide which one is better for you.

The small notes were important because they emphasized another more important note through the use of dissonance. That's why composers, in the true spirit of improvisation, left the duration of the ornamental tone up to the performer.

Let's look at the trill sign:

tr ⌣ ⌣⌣⌣ *tr*⌣⌣⌣

All throughout the Baroque and Classical periods, and not infrequently in Chopin's music, the trill should begin on the note above the main note (the one with the *tr* over it).

Chopin: Mazurka, B flat, Op. 7, no. 1

In all ornaments, the accent falls on the very first note, even though it is short. The notes which follow this first note are played as lightly as possible (wrist raised, fingers hanging down loosely, tickling the keys).

This symbol is the one for a *mordent:*

It looks like the symbol for a trill, except that there is a vertical line through it. The name means biting, and the ornament should "nip" into the main note, without warning. In this example, Bach demands our attention by using a mordent on the very first note.

182

J.S. Bach: Sarabande from French Suite V in G

Speed, pertness and lightness are bywords for playing ornaments. Ornaments are meant to tickle, alert and delight the ear, never to belabor it. It is better to play them with the tips of your fingers, with a flick of the wrist for snappiness. A composer will often place ornaments at the heart of the phrase to draw attention to it.

J.S. Bach: Two-Part Invention, no. 1 in C major

If you see a small note written beside a larger one, it is an *appoggiatura*. If it appears in music written before Beethoven, it is meant to be played on the beat, with the left hand. Here are two kinds of appoggiaturas, short and long.

Mozart: Allegro maestoso, Sonata, A minor (K. 310)

However you feel about ornaments, they are a vital part of early music that cannot be misread or ignored. Study the different ways in which they are used, and you will discover the true beauty of early music.

PRACTICE POINTERS

Little Prelude in C Major

Bar 1: The ties of Bach's bass octave C suggest that he either imagined this, or played it on the organ where the pedal could hold this sound. On the piano, lift your arm *before* playing. Release it easily but completely into the octave C, as if this were an ending, not a beginning.
Bars 2-4: The right hand must play each eighth note very evenly, to start the pulse and build momentum. The *crescendo* must still be very small (*poco*) , as subtle as the grey light of dawn changing to rose. Continue that slight *crescendo* to—
Bars 5-8: The *mf* level, which should be sustained *through* Bar 8.
Bars 9-12: This is like a fresh start (*p*) on a new tonal level (the bass is G, not C as in the opening). That bass G builds suspense through its broken-octave sway, and by the energizing *mordents* Bach adds to each strong beat. The word *mordent,* from the Latin *mordens,* means "biting." Far more structural than "ornamental," these *mordents* must "bite" by accenting their *first*, quick note:

This shuddering little shake suggests power building through the repeated Gs, a tension that must eventually be dispelled in the bass C of the final Bar 16.
Bars 13 and 14: Sustain the *mf* dynamic level, and don't rush the sixteenth notes.
Bars 15 and 16. Again, sustain your *forte* level, the shining "sun-up" our early "dawn" had promised. That is the right way with a piece called "prelude;" it must "bloom" rather late to suggest there's still more to come.

LITTLE PRELUDE IN C MAJOR
FROM "SIX LITTLE PRELUDES"
(SCHMIEDER 939, NO. 1)

J.S. Bach
(1685-1750)

185

Pedaling is "the soul of the piano." (*Anton Rubinstein)* And yet, poor pedaling can bedevil piano playing, and ruin your best intentions.

You should already know something about the three pedals, and, no doubt, the right pedal has had your foot on it more than once. The right pedal is, of course, the *damper pedal* (do not call it the "loud" pedal). It simply raises the dampers from the strings, allowing them to vibrate sympathetically when you play.

The middle pedal (if your piano has one) is called the *sostenuto pedal,* and the left one is the *una corda pedal* (literally the "one string pedal"). The workings of these two pedals will be discussed in the "Syncopated pedaling" section of this chapter. In the majority of this chapter, however, we will only discuss the damper pedal, the one you probably learned to use first, and the one you need the most. If you look under the lid of the grand piano, you will discover that most of the strings have dampers (up to the third E above middle C). Those without are short enough to need their free vibration to fortify their sound.

Test the feel of the damper pedal with your right foot, your heel securely on the floor, and the joint of your big toe against the "toe" of the pedal shape. Next, rhythmically press the pedal down and let it up as you slowly chant:

> Poor pedaling can ruin your best intentions.

Down | Up | Down | Up
de - *press,* | re - *lease,* | de - *press,* | re - *lease.*

This rhythm exercise will teach you how to properly use the damper pedal. Rub your foot into the pedal, and keep your foot on the pedal as you raise it, making no pedal noise as you do.

Here are some common uses of the damper pedal. They are arranged in order, from easiest to learn to hardest to learn.

A. Pedaling with the sound played

1. Sonority Pedal - In this usage, the pedal is pressed to add a pool of sound, enriching an important or long note. The pedal is raised when you wish to end the sound.

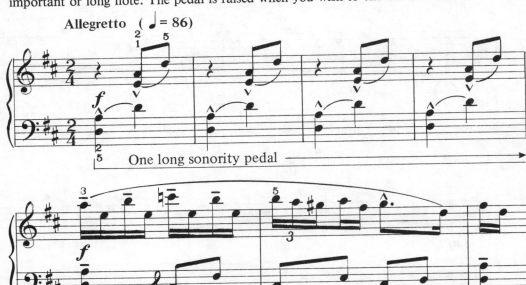

Bartók: Sonatina   © *Copyright 1950 in U.S.A. by Boosey & Hawkes, Inc. Reprinted by permission.*

2. Rhythm Pedal - Here, you pedal only *with* the note you want to stress, usually on the regular strong beats of the meter. For example:

a. Any waltz bass:

b. Any downbeat in 4/4:

Lincke: "Glow Worm"

Be careful that your bass tone is a vital one. This way, we won't hear the pedal "pumping."

3. Punctuation Pedal - In this type, you still press the pedal down and up with the sound played, but this is done only where you want a splash of added sound. This is exemplified by the 32nd piece from Bartok's *Pieces for Children*.

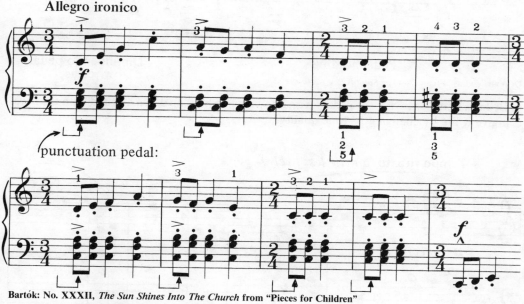

Bartók: No. XXXII, *The Sun Shines Into The Church* from **"Pieces for Children"**

4. Percussion Pedal - There are times when a composer wants a real shock. Since we can't overforce tone production, a deliberate quick press of the pedal adds an inaudible "thump" to the sound, adding to the volume of sound.

187

Beethoven: First movement, Sonata, B flat, Op. 22

(*)

* Slight pedal noise
Helps "cut" sound clean

5. Diminuendo Pedal - This is particularly effective for long sounds, especially at the end of a piece. It allows you to thin the sound by stages. These changes of tone quality, strangely enough, give the illusion of continuing tone.

[LIKE THE SOUND OF DISTANT HORNS ---   MORE DISTANT STILL AND MORE "HELD BACK".]
comme une lointaine sonnerie de cors   encore plus lointain et plus retenu

Pedal holding

Diminuendo pedal —
a slow release

Debussy: ending, Prelude — *The Sounds and Perfumes*

6. Bellows Pedal - Moving the pedal up and down while holding down a sound with the keys can give it life by changing its tone quality.

Tempo rubato *(a little less lively)*

Pedal releases late   "Bellows" pedal

188
Debussy: First Arabesque

B. Syncopated pedaling (or, pressing the pedal down after the sound has been made)

7. Legato Pedal - is applied after you play a sound, in order to enrich the sound and connect it to the next sound.

Legato pedal:

Chopin: Prelude, C minor, Op. 28, no. 20

8. Legatissimo (Overlap) pedal - This type of pedaling deliberately allows one sound to carry over into the next. The clarification of sound that comes with the late pedal release is like a camera lens bringing an image into focus.

* "Overlap pedal"

"G chord "focuses" now.

Ravel: Modéré, Sonatine (1905)

9. The Una Corda (Soft) pedal - is best pressed down *before* you play. It shifts the entire grand piano action sideways, so that each hammer is in position to play two of the three strings for each pitch. Thus, while it softens the sound, it also offers a change of quality: a less rich, dryer sound. For this reason, artists can use it to apply a different tone color to a passage, without having to change their touch.

* *Una corda* pedal here ⟶ (held *through* section as a color-change.)

Schumann: *Knight Rupert,* from Op. 68

10. The Sostenuto (middle) Pedal - This pedal locks the dampers on certain notes, allowing them to ring out while you play oher notes. It must be pressed slowly, well after you have played a sound. This enables the pedal to lock the dampers that are raised. One of its best uses is allowing bass tones to sound through other sounds being played in higher registers.

190

Debussy: *Jardins sous la pluie* **(Gardens in the Rain)**

11. **Degrees of pedaling** may be realized with the damper pedal. A "half pedal" or a "sur-face pedal" permits the dampers to lightly graze the vibrating strings, trimming but not stopping the sound. This changes the tone color, diluting it to a watercolor paleness that allows for longer pedals, as in this example.

* *One* pedal, a "half-pedal", holds *through* Debussy's slur.

Debussy: *Girl with the Flaxen Hair*

Pedal Mixtures - Using one pedal with another in changing combinations can create some delicious mixtures of tone colors. In mixing, artists conform their feet to the rounded shape of the pedals, allowing them to slide sideways without noise. For example, the triplets in the following example might be played with a combination of the *una corda* pedal and the *damper* pedal. Later in the piece, when the triplets return, they can be played without the *una corda* pedal, but with the *damper* pedal.

* *Una corda:* holds through **pp** section.
Damper pedal changes with harmonies while you *hold* una corda pedal.

Schubert: Impromptu, A flat, Op. 90, no. 4 (D. 899)

PRACTICE POINTERS

Prelude in A Major, Op 28., no. 7

Bar 1 to the end: Follow the pedal changes closely. They reflect the richness of the modern bass sonority and clarify the following figure, which led Robert Schumann to call this piece a "slow Mazurka":

Continue, throughout the piece, to change the pedal with the *second* beat of the bar. Bar 2, beat 3: Continue to pedal, every other bar, with that upbeat 3. This is the springy toe-step just before the heel (downbeat) of that "mazurka."
Beat 3: Here and elsewhere, try for the suggested nuances of ——◁ or ▷—— . They represent the changing character vibrating in each harmony as it holds for two bars.

To find the weight balance for these repetitions, in order to maintain an unbroken sound: (1) let your arms hang freely from shoulders to floor. (2) Let them sway slowly, back and forth, still hanging from your shoulders. (3) *As* your *upper* arms continue a slow forward-backward sway, gradually raise your forearms up from the elbows until they hover above the keys they are to play. (4) Still swaying front-to-back from the upper arms, let your forearms sink into the keys, until your continual swaying simply plays the keys and lightly repeats them without a break. Once your arm weight finds its balance at the elbow, the wrist, slightly raised, will seem to "float." The dangling hands will seem to play "by themselves." That is the balanced, passive condition in which you can color your repetitions with the above nuances ——◁ and ▷——

Once you have found such a balance with the keys, try for an overall arc of increasing tension from Bar 1 through Bar 12. Keep the "glow" through Bar 14, and ease away through Bar 15 (without retarding!) to deep repose at Bar 16.
Bars 5, 8, 11 and 15: Give extra tone to the inner voices that are tied.
Bar 12: If you cannot play all of the right-hand chord at once, you may try a rich roll from bass through soprano:

Bar 14: Try the effect of a *half*-pedal on beat 2, *without* losing the bass.
Bar 16, beat 3: Instead of an abrupt clearing of the pedal, try a slow-fade *diminuendo* pedal; that is, a very gradual release. This allows the sounds to "dissolve" into the silence. We're not quite sure where, or whether, the sound has ceased.

PRELUDE IN A MAJOR
OP. 28, NO. 7

Frédéric Chopin
(1810-1849)

194

Mozart, our faithful guide, has seen us through this far. He advised us, after learning the notes in time to "give expression to every note - tastefully and as they are written, *so as to create the impression that the player had composed the piece."* (Author's emphasis)

Does Mozart prescribe an impossible vision of musical conviction and technical ease, of experience and personal well-being, a vision of someone "telling his story" at the piano? I think not, but we will need, once again, to examine our interpretation of Mozart's statement.

The practicing has been well done, and the performer knows the way through a piece of music. He is willing to show the audience, too. He wants to please and delight you, amaze and surprise you with themes, sounds and beautiful things he has discovered as he was practicing the piece.

The artist above, and the artist in every one of us, is a little naive, perhaps childlike. We renew, with an innocent childlike sense of awe, every piece we play, every time we play it. We *must* renew a piece with every repetition.

While in the back of his mind, the practicer can still allow himself a margin for error, the performer must invest himself completely in the present. He must think *"Now* is the moment I have practiced for. I must help them (the listeners) to feel what I have felt, and I must keep them listening. I must build the suspense, so that they fall under my spell and join me in this 'now'."

If that sounds like an incantation, it is worthy and representative of the powerful magic that music can create. In a good performance, time stands still. Each oncoming sound becomes more stirring, illuminating, almost unbearably sweet. These sounds compel us to listen. They seem to collect our scattered energies and make us whole again. After the performance, we leave, renewed and refreshed, ready once again for the "real world."

The artist, working with the composer, can do all this. When you perform, *you are* that artist. This is exactly what Mozart is telling us to be every time we play.

You may be asking yourself "How do I become this paragon performer?" You start by changing your psychology from that of practicing to that of performing. Start with that "newborn" approach to music. Tell yourself that the music you are about to play - no matter when it was composed - is being reborn *now*, under your fingers. With your performance, it is being given another chance to live. Without you, it must hide on shelves among scores of other pieces. Your energy can summon this music to live again *now*.

You should not be intimidated by these thoughts. What matters most in your performance is your ability to resurrect the music. You should not worry about what other people say. People will always say something, but remember that criticisms need not be negative. If you can think objectively about what people say, you can understand their comments. Here you are, doing something on your own, presenting a piece of yourself. Naturally, everyone wants to present something of their own and have it approved. But, for some reason, they are not doing it, perhaps for fear of disapproval. So they are critical of your performance. Rest assured, however, that, if you intend your music as a gift and modestly present it as such, it will be accepted as such. Since it is a gift of yourself, they will be aware of the cost, and will be pleased.

I often discuss the fear of performance because although it is an unreal sort of fear, it can cripple. I know hundreds of musical adults who not only accepted fear as a dimension of performance, but nearly let it overwhelm them when they play for others. The word "nearly," however, is the light at the end of the tunnel. It is the composer's light, bottled up in the music that is clamoring to be set free, much like the genie in Aladdin's lamp. Let out that genie, and liberate yourself at the same time.

To borrow a phrase from the late Eloise Ristad, set free the "performer within" you and *play,* exposing every feeling to the public. Forget those shadowy negatives, and convert them to positive affirmations. When you do, you've already begun practicing for performance. See yourself seated at the piano, among friends, loose and free, being swept along

**IV
PRACTICING
FOR A
PERFORMANCE**

195

with the music, lifted on the waves of sound. You know the road; you've taken the trip many times in your practice. Your physical vehicle - all the skills of technique and expression that you've learned - will carry you safely through. You have trained so you can make this trip. Accept that, and free your mind for the known highlights of the trip. Enjoy them as never before, and let your good self pour forth.

Here are a dozen points to guide your final run-throughs of a piece. Practice these attitudes as you did your notes, and you will be sure to succeed.

1. Play a daily run-through for someone. Schnabel would say "Play for the dog." Regardless of who you play for, play through without stopping. You may drop notes, but don't drop beats.

2. Space your repetitions of the piece. Before playing the piece again, stop and stretch, or better yet, conduct it all the way through.

3. Conjure up the tempo of the piece before you start to play. Think at least two full bars in the tempo, manner and mood of the music, and begin to play in the "third" bar. By then, your sense of time is fully awakened.

4. *Think twice, play once.* Mental rehearsals must equal physical ones at the piano. If you can run through your piece at least once mentally in bed at night, before going to sleep, it can sharpen the signals to your control centers and deepen the impulses from which your musical feelings arise.

5. Set different starting points throughout your piece, giving each a number. In the days before your performance, start at points midway through the piece, in order to give them the freshness of your attention. It also helps to make a "grocery list" of these inner starting points, noting a special feature of each (i.e. - "No. 5: the two hands move one octave higher").

6. Contrasts enliven any narrative, so heighten the contrasts in your pieces: dynamic contrasts, differences between themes, the fresh manner and touch that sets off the start of each new phrase.

7. Repetitions deserve variety, if they are to seem fresh. Decide exactly how you will play each repetition differently the second time.

8. Each piece has a single climax. Stand back, and hum the music. Be sure of where you want to make this climax, and then make it very clear. It is *the* feature that lends interest to the entire musical landscape.

9. Choose your support group. It could be one or two good friends, a sympathetic family member, or even the dog (mine is my canary). What matters is that you have extra ears present. That heightened perception will exhilarate you at the strong places, and help you notice undiscovered weak places.

10. The "Now" psychology must come into your every session at the piano. Use the tape recorder to play back your repetitions. Judge them objectively. Say to yourself "What would I think if this were someone else playing?" Don't forget: *go on* when you play. If there is a hitch, don't let it throw you. Drop the notes, but not the beats. There is no second chance in a performance. You've got to deliver the first time.

11. Remember that you will live to play many more performances. What you will need from your friends are warm but honest reactions. Whatever the verdict about a run-through, smile at yourself. Rack up the good points, and reward yourself for a job well done. Consider the weak points, and sleep on them. Go after them the next morning, and plan for your next performance.

12. *Don't over practice before a performance.* Unspaced repetitions diminish your returns. Study the score silently, and conduct or sing it through. Build your inner conception of the music. Run through the motions *pp* on a table top, but do not squander the energies that will put the fine edge on your performance.

In a good performance, time stands still.

196

AFTERWORD

ith your performance, we've reached a natural pause in practice. Accept the congratulations, for they are in good faith, and accept whatever criticism you can fit into your self-evaluation when you practice next. When you average out the pluses and minuses, give yourself a grade and sleep on it. Remember that your greatest plus of all is the spirit that will drive you to the piano the next day to learn a new piece.

The way music can suddenly well up inside you, or the way good singing or playing can touch you is the evidence of your love for music. That is where your soul is tuned. And that is where this book began, with the love of music that draws you to the piano, and enchants you during practice. They used to say "Practice makes perfect." I suppose that is true enough, but, personally, I'm far from perfect. "Perfect" is the standard which we set up before ourselves, and it is what helps us to grow. It is said that there was a time when even Horowitz had to be encouraged onto the stage with a shove. What sort of paralyzing "perfection standard" was he holding up before himself?

It is better to say that "Practice makes progress," for better practice will certainly give you that. I would give a lot of attention to the practice process that we discussed in the beginning of Part II, for half of the fun is getting there. It is the process of making music that we practice - that fine interplay of mind and matter that sharpens our faculties and brings them into harmony at the same time. In this way, we will surely progress, and grow towards whatever "perfection" lies promised in our stars.

A SIGHT-READING WORKSHOP

Almost everyone is familiar with the three guardian monkeys - see no evil, hear no evil, and speak no evil. They remind me of the three elements of good sight-reading, which combine sight, hearing and touch. If you don't want to monkey around at the keyboard, keep in mind that a good sight reader is guided by what he or she sees (on the printed page), hears (either before or after a note is struck), and feels (on the keyboard).

Hearing is important; ideally your hearing guides your fingers and hands, and keeps them on track. However, the average pianist will perform a little trial and error before finding the right notes. This is often true even for a familiar piece. Take, for example, the melody of "Beautiful Dreamer".

When you arrive at the * and play a *C* or *E* instead of the correct note, something tells you that it is not right. You may try again and play a *B* or an *E flat*. You flush a little, and keep trying to find the right note. When you finally do, you've lost your place on the page!

How can this be avoided? Music reading requires the harmonious cooperation of all three elements: you see, you touch and you hear together. This cooperation will be strengthened through practice, so that you will see and hear recurring patterns and your touch, in turn, will become more accurate.

Touch

Chances are, your sense of touch is weaker than your sense of sight. "Reading" the keyboard is similar to reading Braille, the sequence of tiny bumps which forms letters and words for the blind. A good sight reader feels his way through a piece, not note for note, but handful by handful.

Many people have a quick comprehension of the printed page - of what it "signals" - but are helpless with the keys. They endure considerable frustration in trying to find a key to press for each individual signal. Their eyes do a little dance from page to hand, and the rhythm, musical shape and continuity disappear in the hunting and hesitation. They are spelling their musical words letter by letter!

So we must begin improvement with keyboard feel. The answer is scales! Behind every melody or chord there is a scale, and the feel of that scale is your tactile slide-rule for measuring the correct movements of your fingers.

First, feel the major scales in five finger "slices" up and down the keyboard.

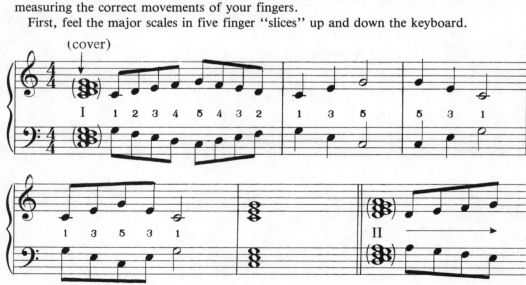

Music reading requires the harmonious cooperation of three elements.

Then, derive the major chords (triads) from these scales, by playing the five note scale, and leaving out the passing notes between chord tones.

Work through the same patterns in all keys, in this order: C, G, F, D, A, E, B, D-flat, A-flat, E-flat, B-flat and finally G-flat. Try to find the notes of each scale by "ear" first. If that doesn't work, you can then fall back on this formula.

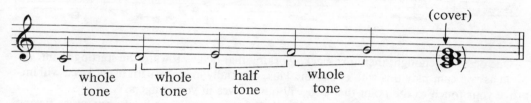

Be patient with yourself. In most everyday activities, whether you are handing someone a pencil or turning a page, your four fingers work *against* your thumb. Scales, on the other hand, ask you to open up the hand partly, then keep it half open while each finger in turn lightly squeezes down its key, then lets go. Your hands may feel a little "thick" at first, simply because you are getting brain signals through to unexplored places!

The next step in familiarizing yourself with the feel of keyboard patterns is to play other types of scales and intervals.

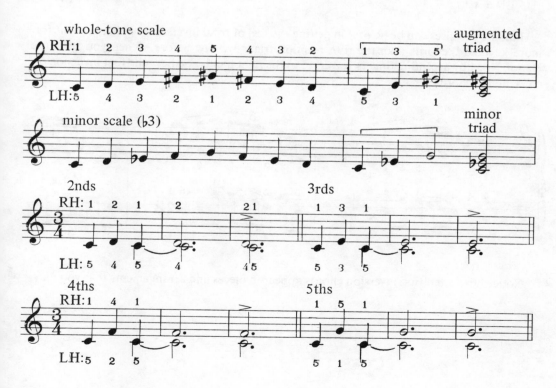

199

Let's continue to develop the sense of touch necessary for good sight-reading with some of Hanon's five finger exercises. Hanon, whom one of my old teachers, Maurice Dumesnil remembered at the Paris Conservatory as the bent and wizened gnome of *La Mecanique,* invented the "escalator clause" in music. His five finger scales "leave out a note, but *not* a finger," which allows the action of the fingers, moving in sequence, to slowly spiral the hand forward on the keys.

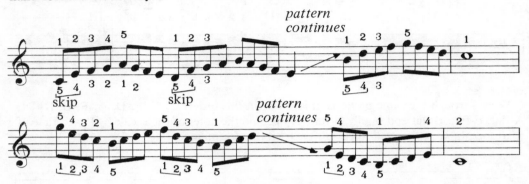

One octave is enough, then turn back, working that octave toward the starting point. As soon as you can, play this with eyes shut. This, especially in scales with black keys, will improve your touch to the point that you will have "eyes in your fingers."

Next, try what I call "Hanon On Wheels," in triplets. They keep your wrist flexing ("breathing"), as you play.

Hanon's exercises can be helpful in getting the feel of triad inversions, which account for more keyboard chords than the root position triads we saw before. When you structure Hanon No. 1 by accenting fingers 1, 2 and 5 in the right hand, you have the first inversion of an A minor chord.

Notice how often first inversion chords appear in pieces and arrangements that you play.

You can tell them by their "gap" - the wider spacing (of a fourth) between the two upper tones:

The upper note of that "gap" is the root, or the *name* of the chord. "Meet me at the top of the gap," I say to my students, recalling to them the *spelling* of the chord they are seeking.

Second inversion chords have their "gap" between the *lower* two notes.

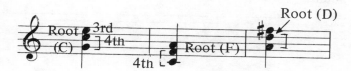

Here is a way to work all triads, in all three positions, into your hands. This will program a large part of piano music into your memory.

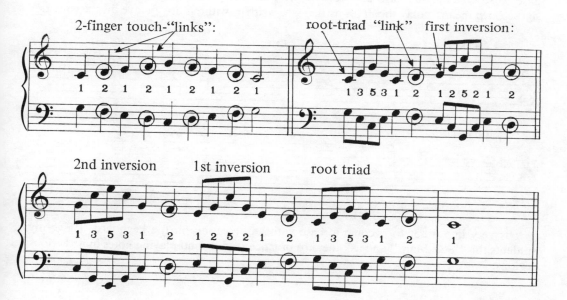

Be patient with yourself. Work slowly, making good tones, and try each of these studies with just one hand first, then with both, moving in both parallel and contrary patterns.

Seeing

Now that we have worked through several exercises to teach your fingertips to feel, and your hand to cover standard shapes and anticipate changing forms, let's begin to examine how printed notes signal your movement on the keyboard.

Each C on the keyboard begins and names an octave. Here are those names.

NAMES OF KEYBOARD OCTAVES

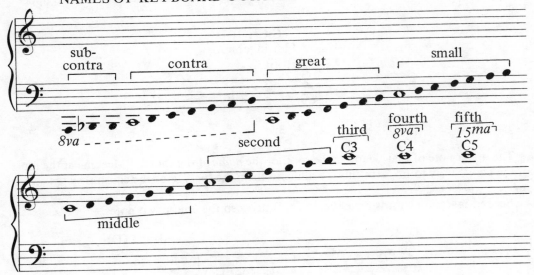

Since the "Grand Staff" roughly corresponds to the full piano keyboard, you should become familiar with any location it charts. Look out for the *8va* (play an octave higher) and *8va bassa* (play an octave lower) signs, with their light dotted lines, which are sometimes hard to see. You should also be aware of the word *loco* which appears after one of these signs. *Loco* means "play the notes as they are written, without any octave displacement."

LOOKS:

SOUNDS:

It is very important to become at ease with any location on the keyboard. I give my students this "Star Map," and ask them to practice reading and playing notes in its various regions.

Practice writing down and playing, in random order, little "star treks" out and back from the landmark notes in the example above. For instance:

Such experiments help you to read steps and skips of a single, horizontal melody line accurately. Pianists, however, are two-handed players, and will want to practice reading and feeling all intervals which lie under the five finger position. We can group intervals on the staff as "likes" (line to line) or "unlikes" (line to space).

"Likes" (line-to-line)

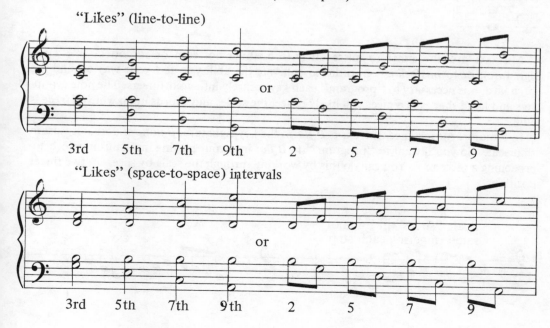

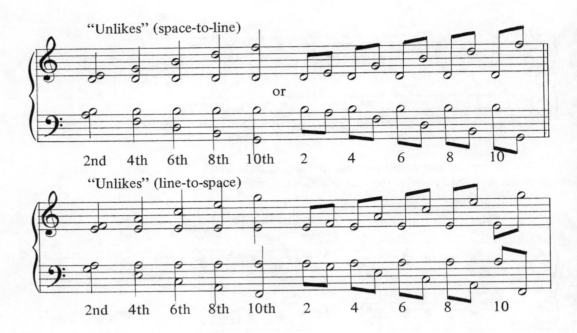

The feeling aspect of this exercise is most important. It is a good idea to play through little progressions such as the following one, without ever breaking off touch with the keys. Hold the common tones (tones which are the same from interval to interval), even if you must substitute another finger to hold a note as you move your hand into position for the next interval.

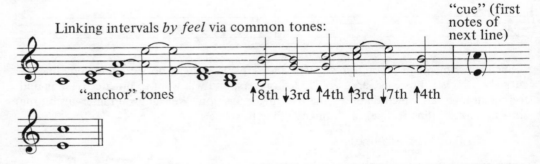

Mistakes are due either to misreadings (something not seen or forgotten, like a key signature), or to *misfeelings*. In order to cultivate the ability to feel your way around the keyboard, it is necessary to "program" each key securely into your fingers. The note groupings and hand shapes in a piece will likely reflect the scales and chords upon which a piece is built.

In F major, for instance, there is a *B flat* in the key signature. *B natural* does not exist in that scale. So you'll want to "program" the *B flat* into your playing mechanism before approaching a piece in F. You can do this by working through the scale by slices, in five finger positions.

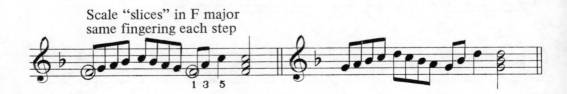

Scale fingering   "slices" with scale fingering

Keep your eyes closed if you can. This will help you experience most of the "handfuls" a composer will present to you in an F major piece. Then, the piece will be just another grouping of patterns placed upon this scale.

The next step is to work on chord inversions. You will see these more often than you will see root position chords! Again, develop a sense of touch, using the following two exercises. Work each pattern one octave up and down each scale.

first inversion   second inversion

Now you are ready for a practical application of the points we have been discussing. Work through the G major chords of Purcell's Prelude before you sight-read it like a pro.

Andantino

Feel and name each chord; notice inversions

Earlier, we worked on spotting the "gap" in each chord. Here, you have begun to combine this *sight* aspect of reading with the *feel* of the notes beneath your fingers.

Now, let's look at the various pitfalls which should be kept in mind when reading a piece.

Accidentals are the sharps (#), flats (♭), and natural signs (♮) which alter any regular scale tone, however briefly. Sharps push a note to the right on the keyboard, flats push a note to the left. Accidentals remain in effect only for the bar in which they appear, and they are cancelled by the barline. This is one of the most forgotten aspects of sight-reading.

For example, in Bach's Little Prelude No. 1 in C major, sharps appear in the left hand in the first bar, and flats in the right hand of the next measure.

"Leans" toward A minor

F major

These alterations - I call them "Promissory Notes" - forecast a new scale or key to come. However, these notes may or may not be "paid." That is, the promised new key or scale may never appear. They do, however, inject variety and expectation into a piece. If you notice the same sharp or flat inserted again and again, chances are that a new key *is* being asserted by the composer.

In order to play accidentals correctly, try to analyze and keep in your mind what is taking place (in terms of possible key changes). In the Bach example above, the sharped notes create a pull toward A major, and the flatted notes create a pull toward F major. Making sense out of accidentals makes them easier to sight-read.

Here are some other things to be aware of when sight-reading:

Repeated Notes - Busy eyes are likely to see them moving up or down instead of staying in one place. You can mark them with a straight arrow as a reminder.

Tied Notes - That second black note-head is very likely going to signal your muscle to play the same note again. A good cure for this is to lightly press the held key at the new beat.

Breaks - At the end of lines, look ahead so that there is no break in the flow of the music from line to line (or lightly pencil in the "cue note" that starts the next line).

Skips - Use the black key groups to keep you in the proper place. "Choreograph" your hand movements in relation to each other.

"Road Closed" Signs - Watch for these warnings of immediate key changes. They usually appear as miniature key signatures at the end of a line.

Register Changes - *Ottava, Ottava bassa, 8va, 8va bassa, col 8* indicate changes of register; the word *loco* restores your playing to the notes as printed.

You will go a long way toward removing these pitfalls to accurate reading by:

1) Surveying the scene (before you play), especially the key signature - the most overlooked of all signals.

2) "Pawing Out" the music, that is, laying it out and experiencing it by handfuls. This will help you find a fingering which is natural to your hands. Try to feel the "handfuls" of the music - the way your hands fall naturally over the keys - so that you will automatically form the physical posture needed for smooth playing.

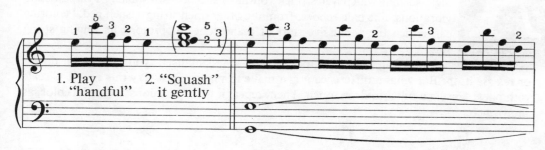

3) Playing freely, with the confidence allowed by "feeling ahead."
4) Listening to yourself, and savoring the continuing sound of each chord.
5) Taking your time. It is most important that you play slowly, and approve each new sound before you move on to the next one.

Keep these elements in mind, and you will never again be afraid to face the music on a new page. Sight-reading can be fun, and these few steps should help to smooth the way to many rewarding moments at your piano.

PIANO PEDAL-GOGY

Anton Rubinstein called the pedals the "soul" of the piano, yet they are often the most neglected and misunderstood aspect of the instrument. Take the right *damper pedal* (sometimes called the *loud pedal*) as an example. When you press it all the way down, it lifts the dampers away from all the piano strings, so that whichever strings you have struck will awaken "sympathetic" vibrations, like pale echoes, from the other open strings. Such pedal coloring can enrich the percussive start of piano tone, or prolong its singing string sound.

The action of this damper pedal is simplicity itself: you can *press* it down, or *release* it up. But what a difference it can make to piano tones. Try this simple C scale with pauses, using a full arm-drop touch. Then, repeat it with "cushions" of pedal color, as shown here:

> *To a quick ear and sensitive toe, dozens of degrees of color can be discovered.*

To a quick ear and sensitive toe, dozens of degrees of color can be discovered between a rich tone deeply pedaled, and tones produced by the gradual release of the pedal through to *diminuendo* fadeaways.

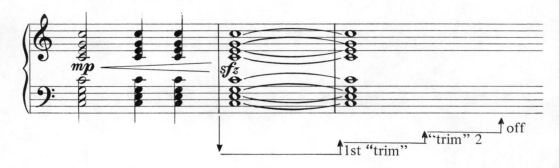

As you release the pedal only partway up, the dampers "graze" (but do not stop) the vibrating strings, changing the sound to one that is purer, or more transparent. It may seem to add "howls" or far-off echoes that you hadn't heard in the full sound. This use of the damper pedal to "shave" or "trim the tops" off the vibrations of the strings will radically change their colors as they continue to sound. The ear, registering a more vital sound, interprets that change as life, continuity.

Recall your high school text on the physics of sound. A string vibrates not with a simple wave, but, rather, with waves-on-waves: a basic long, simple wave-form piled high with increasingly shorter wave shapes.

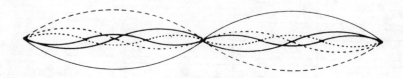

Those top waves - the "upper partials," as we call the higher shaped waves - are the brighter sounds literally "struck" from the strings by the hammer blow. The faster you press down the key, the more these upper partials (tone colors) will respond. They add the flavor to your tone. Musicians call this *timbre*.

Try this experiment: "caress" a key in the middle of the keyboard, "stroking" it down and towards you. Then change your tack: thump it hard; find its point of resistance to your touch, and give it a quick little "jab" at that point. (You may have heard your piano tuner do this again and again, as he searched for those noisy "off-colors" to tune.) With these two touch extremes, you will discover how much tone capacity lurks in even an old, dull instrument, and it will suggest to your ear the vast range of timbres any piano can give you.

You can produce plenty of tone colors with fingers, hands and arms, unaided by the pedals. Remember that the best makeup artists begin with the natural shape and form of the face. Pedal color is the cosmetic of piano playing. It can be merely smeared on, or, with good taste, almost imperceptibly applied to reveal the shape or hidden dimensions of music.

It is important *when*, or *where*, in the "life" of a tone, you apply damper pedal color. For example, if you depress the pedal before you play and then strike a key quickly, you get the fullest, widest response from the piano "harp" - a full symphony of sympathetic vibrations that can give your tone a "sailing power" that nearly obscures its fading. If, on the other hand, you strike the key first, *then* apply pedal after the percussion, you will most likely awaken the strings that "sympathize" at the fourth, fifth or octave: perfect intervals that lend a tone a gentle, purring sheen of sound.

The pedal, in fact, can give you power over the *entire* life of a sound. Depress the damper pedal with (or just before) a big, full sound. Strike a key freely and repeatedly, and then "shave" the resulting thunder of overtones by carefully letting the pedal rise part of the way up, so that some of the layered waves of vibration (the upper partials) are stopped, while the fundamental long, strong waves remain. This tactic can create wonders of resonating colors - like shouting up a steep-walled canyon.

Deciding when to pedal even one sound is not guesswork. For that reason, you had better know the piece "cold," before you decide where pedal color can help to further reveal its character.

You can not simply dab on pedal "paint." Pedal power, like fire, is a resource to be used with caution. Use it for "bone" tones (the strong, supportive tones, like the ones at (*) rather than for subordinate material, as here:

short pedal
"tap"

Beethoven: Sonata, F, Op. 10, no. 2

Or, if you will, use it cosmetically, like a good makeup artist, to enhance a telling feature (*) of the music:

Mozart: Fantasy, D minor (K. 397)

Or use it for a total change of mood, as in this daring bit of Beethoven. This is his own pedal marking which he reportedly said should sound "as if heard in a tomb, or vault."

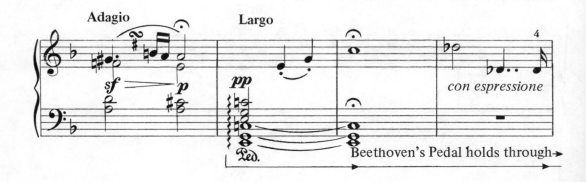

Beethoven's Pedal holds through→

Beethoven: Sonata ("The Tempest"), D minor, Op. 31, no. 2

Holding the pedal longer can add a splash of watercolor to a harmony, letting its sound spread.

Kabalevsky: *The Horseman*

The echoing E octaves in Beethoven's *Für Elise* are best played with a half pedal.

Beethoven: *Für Elise*

With a little experimentation, you will discover how very slight lifts of the foot can produce a veritable rainbow of changing tone colors.

A more active colorization of sound is the "bellows pedal," which, like its namesake, "fans" the sound like a fire and makes it glow. To apply it to big sounds that are supposed to surge onward, rather than fade away, pump the pedal up and down on a beat - usually more than once.

Beethoven: Sonata ("Moonlight"), C# minor, Op. 27, no. 2

The mind will interpret any change in a big sound as movement, even as *crescendo,* though we can physically prove that the holding vibrations are declining in intensity. The following example demonstrates how the bellows pedal can assist Chopin's effect of an organ swell. How else can we interpret his own *crescendo* indication marked below the last harmony of this Nocturne?

212

Chopin: Nocturne, E flat Major, Op. 55, no. 2

These are all structural uses of the pedal that highlight sounds which represent "pillars" of the music, or punctuate the flow of musical ideas. Such a "punctuation pedal" can be used as a dramatic underscore.

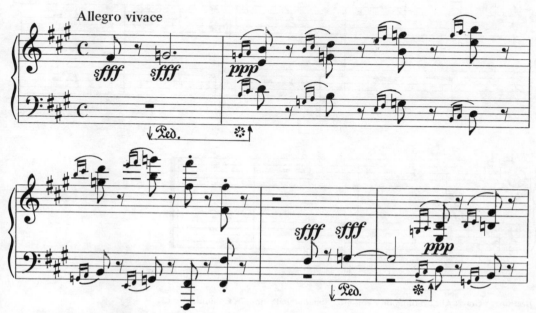

Rachmaninoff: *Polichinelle*, **Op. 3, no. 4**

This type of pedal can also be used to deepen a pause with quiet suspense (despite the marked rest), as many pianists do here:

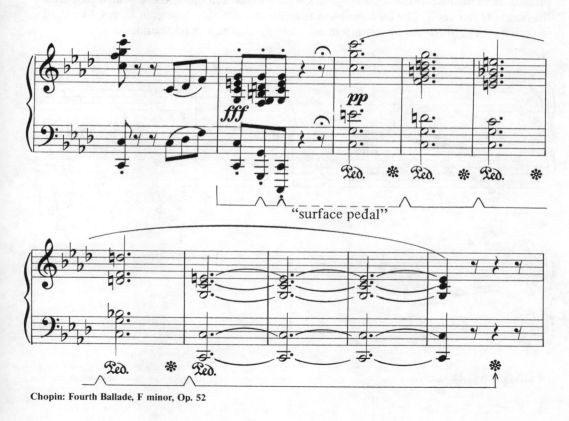

Chopin: Fourth Ballade, F minor, Op. 52

The "percussion pedal" is used to add its own noise to a sudden, loud sound - like a "bark" that bounces off the walls, followed by shocked silence, as here:

Beethoven: Grave: Allegro di molto e con brio, Sonata ("Pathétique"), C minor, Op. 13

The "thump" that we permit (*) with the pedal release helps to cut the reverberations of the sudden, big sound, so that the ear can experience the impact of silence.

Somewhat related to this "percussion pedal" is the "echo pedal," which is first depressed, then held while the sound is struck with a quick and biting force (which rebounds the hand off the keys). The hammer blow reverberates the open strings in waves, like wind in the chimney. Much contemporary music calls for this raw, wild sound:

down before, held *after* sound

S. Bernstein: "The Sea Gull" from *The Birds*   *Used by permission of G. Schirmer, Inc., publisher and copyright proprietor.*

Debussy often asks for an "echo pedal."

This long pedal leaves piano an open "harp"

Debussy: *Jardins sous la pluie* (Gardens in the Rain)

Chopin, of course, teased and played on the piano's overtones like no one else. Consider how the "echoes" he awakens in beats one and two of bar 19 create a fierce energy, and how startling it is when you cut this effect short by cleanly pedaling on beat three:

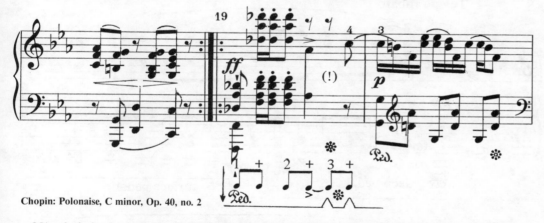

Chopin: Polonaise, C minor, Op. 40, no. 2

Now let's look at an impressionistic effect I call the "howl" or "wind" pedal, which is often lightly applied during a rapid run (not at its beginning or end).

Beethoven: *Für Elise*

Debussy's piano music is perhaps where you most often need a light, surface pedal color, held throughout each musical shape. Debussy also asks for a "cloud pedal" when he writes long bass tones impossible to hold, because your hands are busy elsewhere.

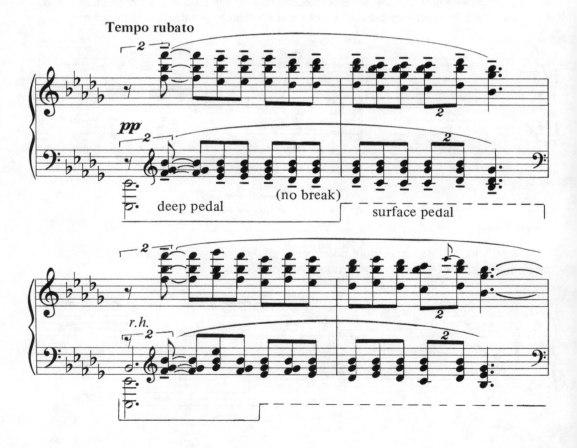

216

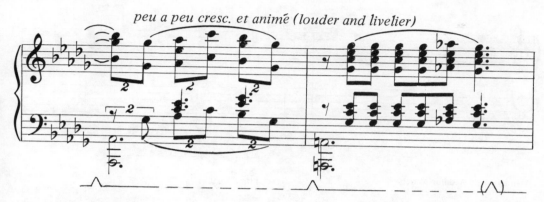

peu a peu cresc. et animé (louder and livelier)

Debussy: *Clair de Lune*

Debussy intends for the damper pedal to be lightly held everywhere. This is because he neither had nor wanted the sostenuto pedal (middle one); its selective spotlight on a single bass tone or tones was unsympathetic to his intention of having columns of overtones seemingly rise directly from the bass.

Debussy's pianistic grandfather, Chopin, is often well served by a light spray of pedal "mist:"

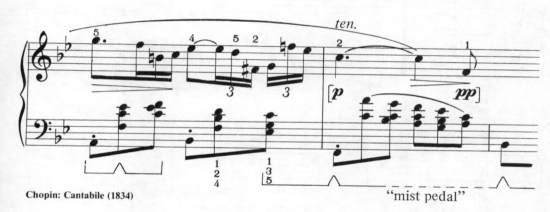

Chopin: Cantabile (1834)   "mist pedal"

These are all ways to group sounds into shapes. Another way to achieve this end is through bold use of the "overlap pedal *(legatissimo pedal)*." In this case, you apply a deep pedal and hold it through both the first and part of the second sound, clearing it while you still hold on to the second sound.

clear pedal changes

Mendelssohn: Wedding March

"overlap pedal"

By far, the most common example of foot and hand coordination is the straightforward "Rhythm pedal." What would you do here if no one told you about pedaling? You would do what was natural - you would "keep time."

Joplin: *The Entertainer*

That regular injection of pedal sound lends buoyant energy to the bass on the downbeat, while releasing the pedal with the second beat gives it added life also.

Beethoven-Busoni: Ecossaises

If, in a dance, the harmony allows you to prolong your "rhythm pedal" a little longer, the later liftoff makes the dance rhythm more lilting.

J. Strauss, Jr.: *The Beautiful Blue Danube*

Contrary to what seems to be a law, the pedal-energized rhythmic stress does not have to always fall on the downbeat.

finger pedal   foot pedal

Schubert: Impromptu, A flat, Op. 142, no. 2

Notice how Schubert never fails to support his "dancers." He gives the bass downbeat a "finger pedal," which holds for three beats. This suggests that you should stress it somewhat, to carry it through the bar (and give the offbeat accent something to react to).

One word of caution! Never let your rhythm pedal degenerate to a mechanical pump that stresses every downbeat to the same degree. Music - especially dance music - groups itself in phrases of several bars each. They are musically strong bars which alternate with one or more weak bars (the weak bars ride along on the impetus created by the strong bar). For our last example, Chopin's *Minute Waltz* goes a long way before making even a slight "touchdown" to earth (*). It would never do to "ground" it with too much excess baggage!

Chopin: Valse ("Minute"), D flat, Op. 64, no. 1